Also by Mary Hamilton

✧*Leaving My Father's House*:

A Journey to Conscious Femininity with Marion Woodman

✧*Under the Horse's Ass*:

A Love Story, Human and Divine

✧*The Dragonfly Principle*:

An Exploration of the Body's Function in Unfolding Spirituality

STILL BORN

Stepping into the Unknown

A Memoir of Dying with My Daughter

MARY HAMILTON

Published in the United States by Colenso Island Press
ISBN: 978-0-986-0936-4-7
1. Memoir 2. Death & Dying 3. Spirituality 4. Non-dual Awareness

CONTENTS

"One way or another the world is going to be made a single, whole entity. It will be unified either in mutual mass destruction or by means of mutual human consciousness. If a sufficient number of individuals can have the experience of the coming of the Self – i.e. the reconciliation of the opposites within their own psyches - as an individual, inner experience, we may just possibly be spared the worst features of its external manifestation."

–Edward Edinger *(Archetype of the Apocalypse,* p. 174)

"The New Story emerging in quantum physics tells us that the whole universe is a unified field. Our lives are part of a cosmic web of life which connects all life forms in the universe and on our planet. Every atom of life interacts with every other atom, no matter how distant. We are not only connected through the Internet but through the infinitesimal particles of sub-atomic matter. We are part of an 'Infinitude of Consciousness' which sustains not only our world, but the entire universe. This restores the original cosmology of the Great Mother at a new level of understanding."

–Ann Barring (*The Dream of the Cosmos: A Quest for the Soul*)

"Death is not extinguishing the light: it is only putting out the lamp because the dawn has come."

–Rabindranath Tagore

"What will life be? It will be a thousand deaths longing for my true life and dying because I do not die."

–St. John of the Cross

"The privilege of a lifetime is to become who you truly are."

–C. G. Jung

AUTHOR'S NOTE

"The name that can be named is not the true name."

–Tao-te Ching

The raw material for *Still Born* is from a journal I kept while sitting with my dying daughter, Laura. The journal faithfully kept my secrets safe from the eyes of the outside world. Writing kept me honest, inviting me to face the truth and uncover my real values. The only way for me to move through life's challenges was for me to digest the 'dung with the gold,' to face my fears, dig deeper, and endure the suffering. The process eventually uncovered the 'gold in the dung'. (Carl Jung)

Once lived, true heart values were released into my awareness. Though my material remains intensely personal, my intimacy with the death of my child presented an invisible key to access my deepest, most intimate core. I recognized the gift, 'the pearl beyond great price,' (Bible) an intense intimacy with the whole of the Life/Death reality.

Eight years later, I am motivated to share my insights, gleaned from unwrapping this unasked for gift.

Some words in the text need clarification. Colenso appears frequently as the soul home where my family spends every summer. Like migrating birds flying north, we drive to the town of Parry Sound, Ontario and then take the boat 17 miles through small channels. Eventually we enter the wide open space of Georgian Bay and there, our beloved island Colenso awaits us. For us, this is sacred land, 'God's country,' though the word God rarely appears in this book.

Historically, a fundamental premise in Christian dogma concerns Father God and his son, the Universal Presence of Loving Light that traditionally overlooks woman's reality, alive in the female body that birthed the god-son. As a girl and teenager, I absorbed the platitudes, rules, and values of Christianity. I feared my body's instinctual life with its 'untamable nature'. I unconsciously idolized the unattainable holiness of the Virgin Mary alongside the visible perfection of beauty in movie stars. However, as a woman born in 1946, a year after the end of World War II, I was not aware of my cultural conditioning as a woman. The shift from Universal Divine Light to individual living light cannot happen unless I identify with the organic sacredness of my woman flesh. Otherwise, part of me will always remain unconscious and outside the field of spiritual wisdom. *Still Born* explores the discernment between what I inherited as a western-educated woman and the true nature of woman's flesh. The lingering image of holding my dead daughter in my arms leads me to ponder the experience of the Virgin Mary story and the image of her holding her dead son, Christ.

The wisdom gleaned from inner exploration expresses a truth that is not mine, but rather resonates through all that I am as living flesh. Then I know I am an incarnate fragment within LIFE, capable of resounding aspects of it. Wholeness includes my daily personal ego life, insights into my spiritual Life, moments of eternal LIFE, and ultimately the reality of my daughter's death.

My intention is to show an inherited human capacity to experience individual uniqueness while abiding in the invisible spaciousness of spirit. The universality of my personal experience presents a more objective viewpoint. Death, once truly known, untethers me from the experience of a separate self. I am a kite flying high in the winds of spirit; and, I am firmly held in beloved hands tenderly touching raw grief. Death roots me deeply into the earth's nature. My intimate awareness stretches my reality between earth's darkness and the sun's radiance. Expanding in all directions, I dwell in vaster, more encompassing fields of the human experience where ancient voices sing their song of truth while secretly conveying a reason for my being.

My hope is to help lessen fears around death and dying. The sanitization of the dying event makes it difficult for loved ones to face the suffering of a dying beloved or feeling the depth of grief. Perceiving with a curious mind associated with death opens the heart to a deeper, richer potential within our human condition. Death, once faced as part of all Life, frees me to taste eternal LIFE, while still born.

I also wish to support others who seek to explore beyond the collective voice to pursue their own uniqueness, thereby unveiling a more profound meaning for life. I hope that my personal investigation of the intimate experiences of birth, life, death, and rebirth, will contribute to the unfolding awareness of the larger human condition.

"Pioneers are always needed, those souls who have the strength and courage to forge ahead into the new. They are the ones who hold that vision ever before them and see it unfold."

—Eileen Caddy, co-founder of the Findhorn Foundation

PROLOGUE

"To end suffering, you must touch the world of no birth, no death."
–Sufi saying

"There is no greater agony than bearing an untold story inside you."
–Maya Angelou

1983 Dream

I am in a golden field, walking towards an old man. I carry the bones of a slaughtered life.

"Old Man," I say. "I have come to bury these bones."

"Yes," he says, "I have been waiting for you."

"What am I to do?" I ask him.

"Bury the bones in sacred soil," he says, pointing to the open field. Then wait.

"Whose bones are they?"

"Yours," he answers. "They are the bones of the mother who gave birth to the dead child, the son sacrificed to awaken you. Life will demand more of you when you realize your truth. The

*part of you that grieves now and in the future is
to be returned to earth. This is your destiny."*

2020 Meditation

"I did not ask for this soul-assignment."

"Yet, here you are, today."

"No wonder I didn't want to be born. No wonder Laura screamed at birth. Who wouldn't yell knowing her destiny?"

"Focus on your own destiny. You are her mother, the one to raise her, nourish her with your heart's blood and life's breath."

"And watch her die in pain! How could you make me be born again?"

"This life is yours to live and our offering to humanity."

"It feels too cruel. I won't re-experience the pain again. I won't."

"But Mary, you have already lived the pain and you survived. Now you know the gift, "the pain of too much loving" (Kahlil Gibran). You know your flesh is of love, the substantiation of an all-loving Being. Remember writing that? Be it. It is your time."

"I don't have the courage."

"Of course, you do. You have incarnated with the strength to endure suffering. Trust what your woman's flesh lives and knows. Engage muted intelligence. The truth of your experience speaks to a universal depth of motherlove, a portal to the Great Love that mystics and sages have lived throughout the ages. Offer that to your world."

Final Vision 2021

I return to the golden field. Walking towards the old man, he smiles, bowing his head in respect. In silence we acknowledge the great abyss. Our bodies, slightly opaque, appear as cut-outs of suspended light. I cradle ancient bones in my arms like a mother holding her beloved infant. The old man watches me as I lovingly drop the polished bones into the bottomless abyss. I am crying in self-awareness. My saltwater tears form into crystals of rainbow colours.

Now I am capable of taking responsibility for the universal nature of my earthly body, made visible in time and saturated with celestial spirit. I am a golden field of boundless space, an old man, an aging woman, liberating her polished bones into the light of an abyss, and I am rainbow crystals of saltwater prisms released from the ocean of human grief. The totality is beautiful with LIFE—I AM a holy place, a self-aware Cathedral, sensuously fleshed as woman, transparent, luminous and still born.

2022 Reflection

Unknowingly, Life dances me into itSelf. I, Mary, is no more. I wake up to realize I am dancing Life.

I am the dancer doing this dance, and yet I am not the choreographer. Life informs me I am rooted in the soul-soil of Mother Earth, my original place of birth, a threshold where life and death collaborate in mutual respect for all life—visible and invisible.

I danced long before I had words. Now I write. The dancing self knows life because she is 'the dance'. As a trained classical dancer, I sense/feel where and what steps I am to make. I write to articulate what my nonverbal self has lived since birth and intimately knows. If I shift attention from conventional thinking, re-focus inside the void and reach up to the light-filled sky, everything changes in quality. I recognize I AM being danced into existence. Once realized; it becomes apparent what my next step is to be.

The material in *Still Born: Stepping into the Unknown* is my heartfelt attempt to articulate a transformation that occurs in human awareness when the skill to shift attention develops into a discrete capacity. After years of disciplined practice as a dancer, teacher, meditator and writer, the veil between life and death, form and formlessness, visible and invisible, becomes porous. Egoic-based skills and pure awareness flow into seamless patterns where the particular and the universal simultaneously arise, conjoin and dissolve as in a dance. I am dancing molecules gathered into a form at birth, and I am still born.

I have practiced crossing through the veil for many years. As a trained dancer I know the qualities living inside the beauty of form; the sense of melting into great love; of being tenderly shaped by energy folding my body into a discrete shape, exquisitely articulated in a dance studio or on a stage. I challenge myself now to uncover word-labels to articulate the dynamic experience of being inside living fields of incarnation. These words become my vehicle to describe my experience of awakening:

> *There is a grief so—utter—*
> *It swallows substance up—*
> *Then covers the Abyss with*
> *Trance—*
> *So memory can step*
> *Around—across –upon it—*
> *As one within a Swoon—*
> *Goes safely—where an open eye—*
> *Would drop Him –Bone by Bone.*

–Emily Dickinson

"Life beyond extinction."

–Sufi saying

1

ROUND ONE, THE SHOCK

"Be patient toward all that is unsolved in your heart and try to love the questions themselves…do not now seek the answer which cannot be given you because you would not be able to live them, and the point is to live everything. Live the questions now. Perhaps you will then gradually, without noticing it, live along some distant day into the answer."

–Rainer Maria Rilke, *Letter to a Young Poet*

May 21, 2008

John and I wake up at the island, innocently assuming all will unfold as we planned. He assumes we are joining our daughters in Toronto for his 65th birthday: I know all the adult cousins eagerly await his arrival for the big celebration—today John becomes an official senior citizen. Let the celebrations begin!

Driving just north of Toronto, the cell phone rings in my purse. Scrambling to find it, I see it is

Laura calling. She must be on her way to Toronto. But she is crying: "I have a lump in my breast, Mommy. They tell me its cancer. I'm at the hospital for more tests. But I will be at Daddy's party, I promise. I might be a few minutes late. No, please don't come to London."

John hears my response. The car creeps into the city with the rest of the parking lot traffic. His focus freezes: "I've gone stone cold," he whispers in shock.

"I've gone numb."

Two stone statues drive into a wall of the unthinkable. Laura arrives at the restaurant just as we sit down for dinner. Her radiance stuns me. The soft auburn curls of her long hair flow gracefully over youthful shoulders, hair she will grow for kids with cancer to make them wigs. The party is a great success.

Finally, we are alone. Lying in bed, holding hands, we blindly stare at a blank ceiling. Through tears, I hear John say, "Why her? She is too young. She is at the peak of her life. Why not me? I have lived my life. I don't need any more. Why can't I give her my life?"

In my shattering heart, a voice keeps repeating, "Will I be able to love her enough?"

May 30, 2008

Laura is at our home for dinner. After spending her week researching various types of cancer, she tells us that, at 28, her chances of survival are grim.

"Oh, darling, I wish I were a god and could fix everything for you."

"I don't want you to be god, Mom. You would be biased. This is my destiny. Let me live it."

Her destiny? Later in bed the words of Gilbran echo through my skull: "Your children are not your children. They are the sons and daughters of Life's longing for itself." The anarchy of words form into painful knots in my heart; clarity fades, chaos rules as my know-it-all teacher self splutters away in my head: "Our human challenge is to live the wound and the healing simultaneously without judgement or denial of death"…"The natural world gives the wound and the capacity to heal, the itching poison ivy and the relieving juice of jewelweed."…"Knowing the Absolute within you gives rise to Being-ness, not as an idea but as a dynamic flow of a creative Life. We open to new sensibilities capable of enduring personal human suffering."….blah…blah…blah...

Words unnerve me; meaningless platitudes; noise clamoring to soothe me when all I feel is life's cruelty. My lord, at 28, surely, she has she been through enough with her beloved fiancé, Tim, dying just four years ago? I visualize being rocked in the loving arms of my soul friends until the arrival of sleep.

I wake up: What if Laura dies? Panic…I go to my meditation room, light my candle, and focus on my breath. An image forms in the silence: A purple radiance pierces down my spine and lands at the base. A voice speaks through the space:

"Laura will die and transform into a much vaster Being."

"NO! I want her to live in this world. I will not let her die!" I force myself to visualize her in healing light. I start praying for her wholeness. I don't know if I am praying. I am begging. I sense-feel a bolt of white light traveling down the inside of my spinal cord. It gathers into an image of a water-lily bulb. What kind of flower is this star-bulb? What seeds does it carry in its invisible core?

Early in the morning I dream:

I need to stay in my kitchen where the heat of the stove keeps me warm. It is a new house I do not recognize. In the living room, Christmas presents are wrapped, waiting to be opened. I must not forget to open them.

Laura comes to sleep in her childhood bed for the next two days of tests. Prayer circles around the world form as our friends light candles in their places of worship and sacred altars in their homes.

Do I really believe in an invisible love that could heal Laura? Or, is it just a comforting thought? I must face my fear. Laura can't deal with my panic on top of all that she must endure. Deep inside I sense an invisible heart connection to other parents who witness their child's pain. Is this the pain of too much love? Life and death meet in the present, deeply intimate moment. An inner feeling of compassion arises within me, compassion for my family and our shared human condition. Looking out the window, I notice the fullness of spring blooming in the city. I am thankful for the beauty and the love of friends, but there is no harmony between my inner reality and the beauty outside my window.

2

DIAGNOSIS AND SURGERIES

"No tree, it is said, can grow to heaven unless its roots reach down into hell."

–C. G. Jung

June 6, 2008

In the Cancer Clinic, all the patients are old and grey, except for Laura. She doesn't carry their shocked, defeated look; rather, she is pissed, deeply sad, and somewhat curious. As she walks into the consultation room, Dr. J recognizes Laura, the camp director his young kids adore, Laura, the director who reads the children's books she writes to the campers at bedtime, Laura, the director who cries sometimes because she misses her beloved Tim who died too soon.

Holding her hands Dr. J makes eye contact: "I am here to do whatever you want me to do for you, Laura." He gently eases her in a chair: John and I sit against

13

the far wall in two white plastic chairs. Dr. J outlines the aggressive nature of her cancer and explains why a complete mastectomy is necessary. I watch Laura's sadness as she realizes the mutilation about to occur. After a long pause, she looks into his eyes: "Is this for you to feel that you have safely done what your expertise has taught you? Reconstruction may look great, but my fake breast will have no feeling, none of my life force."

He listens. Recognizing her need as a young woman for a partial mastectomy, he explains the process. A few surgeries may be necessary to attain clear margins around the tumor. When the margins are clear six chemo drips, three weeks apart, will be necessary followed by 25 daily radiation treatments.

Laura asks: "May I see my MRI and Ultrasound images?" To her delight a screen on the wall becomes a teaching center. He invites her questions arising from her research. He takes time to ponder before answering. She is engaged, alert, interested, and curious. When she learns something new, her humor and radiant joy fill the consulting space with palpable love. As Dr. J explains the surgical procedure in detail, John and I remain silent. Waves of fear roll through my solar plexus. A cavernous hole grows inside me.

Energy drains out. Will I pass out? I grip onto the cheap plastic chair and focus on Dr. J's hands. I try to visualize golden light emanating from them.

When we leave the consulting room, the secretary schedules day surgery for the following Thursday. We drop Laura off at Hobbit House, the playful name she calls her home.

At night I dream:

> *I meet John on an unknown beach. Huge cliffs appear behind us. I realize if the tide is too high, we will drown in grief.*

I must be mindful. But how can I endure grief living in every cell of me and witness what is yet to be?

I fall back on the years of inner work that I started in 1976 after Christopher's stillbirth. I was 30 then, and now 32 years later, destiny knocks me out again. I try to manage the panic around the possibility of Laura's death. I focus on my breath and am thankful the next inhale arrives. I witness my ribs expand and release with air until I feel my heart relaxing. I remember in 1980 when I first walked the labyrinth at a BodySoul Rhythms workshop in California. I sensed a capacity to expand in two directions simultaneously: the forward-backward horizontal direction and the up-down vertical direction. During the time I walked the labyrinth's twisting path, I experienced an intimate, vital nexus where the two directions merged in my heart. I knew this center could endure the stretching between opposing realities, between chaos and order. Now, I question: Will this center hold? Will I be able to love her enough to be present for her, even if she dies? Is this not the same question I asked when she was born prematurely 29 years ago? Can I love her even if she dies tonight? In the hospital that night I meditated. By morning I knew I loved our no-name baby Hamilton, whether she lived or died. I simply loved her tiny body totally. Unconditional motherlove lived me then. When the spontaneous vision of the rainbow linked my heart to hers in our separate hospital rooms, I knew I would take my precious baby home.

Now, the tension of fear overtakes me. John ages before my eyes. His face is puffy with grief. Melissa calls nightly from Toronto. Laura loves her big sister dearly and openly shares with her. All Laura asks of us is this: "Support me and don't get angry when you disagree with my decisions out of your fear that I will die". Every morning, Laura walks 40 minutes along the river path to work at the university. John picks her up and brings her home for dinner. If she has an early doctor's appointment, she stays with us; if not, she returns to Hobbit House. We drive her to all appointments. She inspires us with her positive determination. From her research before each appointment, she asks insightful questions. She walks with intelligent dignity, humor, and presence, bringing love into every consultation room, and tears to every doctor she engages with. The night before her first surgery, Tim's parents fly in from Calgary to be with their "sweet Laura". Like Laura, they still grieve the loss of their beloved son. Like us, they love Laura as their own daughter. As they drive off, Laura weeps in our arms:

"I want a man in my life and not parents. Just cut the fucking boob off and give me my life back."

Eight hours of hell in the hospital today. Tumor out; larger than anticipated; two-week wait for biopsy results. We drive home in silence to the sound of Laura's weeping. Melissa greets us at home, ready to tend to her sister's needs. Upstairs, I hear the music of their laughter as Melissa helps her sister. I go to the basement and cry. What if she dies? I am running around on automatic pilot. I don't recognize my life. My tear ducts won't close; but, when I hear their laughter from the kitchen, automatic pilot blissfully closes them. Something walks this empty shell upstairs and finishes making dinner.

After a few days home, Laura and Melissa return to Hobbit House to be together before they return to work. We drive north to the island, Colenso. The diversion of summer living gives us the appearance of a normal life. I dream I am chewing diamonds.

I wake up in darkness to the sound of John crying in his sleep. By morning I am the tense shell, holding a raging storm inside. I try to visualize golden fields of hope, but hope for what—miracles of healing; a normal life for Laura? Is this her destiny? How can I meditate on still, clear waters and mountain strength when the wrath of an inner storm releases its fury in endless crying? Anger cries out: "I want my life back! Fuck cancer! It is her cancer and not mine!" I feel helpless and overwhelmed. I walk a shaky line between hope and despair, anger and love.

July 10, 2008

We drive back to the city to accompany Laura to the hospital. Dr. J tells her the cancer is metastasizing. She requires more of everything—more surgery, chemo, and radiation. On the way home she phones the university. The Human Resources chairwoman tells Laura she doesn't want to lose her. When her treatments start, Laura will have an unlimited health leave, full salary and all benefits. Quietly, we celebrate Melissa's 31st birthday at a local restaurant. Laura shares her treatment ideas based on her internet research. After dinner, we separate into our respective lives—Laura to Hobbit House and work; Melissa to Iceland with friends; John and me to the island.

That night I dream:

An unknown Chinese woman serves me tea. I share with her my hope that Laura accepts traditional medical treatments followed by alternatives.

Back at the island we hear the unnerving yipping of a wolf pack on a hunt. One morning I watch a terrified fawn desperately swim from island to island, compelled by an instinct to survive. The doe must have offered herself to the circle of howling predators in her attempt to save her child. Is this the same instinctual motherlove in me?

A new stillness grows inside me, a quiet form of paralysis, like a deer caught in the head lights of an oncoming car—paralyzing terror. Will I live in frenzied activity like the fawn in my dream and driven by an unconscious survival instinct? Or, will fear paralyze me into stone? I can't save Laura. Oh, how I long for the refuge of death, the space of the unborn self, where all suffering ceases. Why can't I merge into the eternal moment of infinite peace? I want to live beyond this personal suffering, beyond fear, beyond the ache in my gut. A quiet terror in my gut explodes: "Wake up! Death space is suicide."

Laura needs to have her own life, separate from us. It is better for us, too, to be with friends our own age, drink wine, laugh, be separated from cancer, and live our senior lives. I like identifying with our daughter's accomplishments. All parents love to brag about their smart and talented kids and grandkids. I want normalcy back!

Sometimes I see the beauty of nature surrounding me and feel a flicker of joy—never hope. When I join my cousins in my red kayak for a long paddle into the cool headwinds off the Georgian Bay, I focus on the wave patterns to navigate safely through a watery path. I see the dancing diamonds of light on the waves and know I am in beauty…but I am in pain.

Will I ever realize a reality beyond my unconscious habitual egoic patterns of false hope, magical thinking, and projections? I catch myself begging for help, like a lost child. In the past I have felt a visceral strength, capable of accepting reality as it is—truth in the moment. It protected me, prevented me from acting out like a wild animal in pain. But I was not facing death—Laura's death. I tell myself not to think I ought to be capable of being something I am not. Such effort breeds more suffering.

Laura calls. Another surgery date is set for mid-July to reach clear margins. Tim's sister arrives from Calgary to stay with her at Hobbit House. She needs friends, not Mom and Dad. We stay at the island until the day before the surgery.

A deep sorrow invades the growing silence between us. Alone in my kayak I yell into the empty space: "Damn you, god. Fuck your bullshit about a loving godhead. You are not the big ass creator but a fucking mean-hearted bastard. I hate you! I want to kill you!" Pulling hard on my paddle I realize I have not even thought of Laura, her fear, her sense of loss—and John's—and Melissa's—and then it is all too much. Rage and curses turn to tears and despair. My insatiable inner child-self, fearing the unknown, wants events to change, to be fixed according to my wants and little needs. My adult-self, knowing I can't change the situation, feels helpless. I crave the red-hot strength I feel when I am *really* angry. Strength, anger, frustration, helplessness, despair…a vicious, looping inner soup.

Dread pounds against the shores of my ribcage. A buttress of tension holds me up, ready to face a future most parents can't imagine. Will my heart break into heart failure? Or could it possibly break apart into other possibilities? Is this learning to travel in two directions simultaneously? I dream:

> *I am catching fish and bringing them into the*
> *kitchen. A voice speaks: "Drowning in your*
> *suffering, you disconnect from all that you love."*

Sitting in the rock garden this morning, pulling weeds, a voice whispers in my heart: "Your greatness knows there is no separate you. The egoic-I forgets she lives inside this inner sphere of potential. She drowns in her personal little-me experiences. She cannot digest the experience of losing Laura. You are too attached to being her mother. Attend to the feeling-sense of beauty's pulsating LIFE surrounding you, in you, through you, the pulse of ONE dynamic presence. Awaken to this Self-igniting universe. Awaken. Your gift of motherlove is the capacity to give and to receive simultaneously. Be this radiance generating within you, a self-igniting star that cannot die." Who is this voice of inner wisdom?

The morning we leave for the city to be with Laura for her next surgery, I remember my dream:

I tell John that the fish are coming
home. I am deeply joyous.

Compensation?

July 17, 2008

I do not know if I am weeping in sorrow or in recognition of the sheer beauty of LIFE's mystery. Facing life, facing death, facing reality, facing the gift of our loving family unit can be overwhelming. Another day of surgery is set for tomorrow to get clear margins and obtain a lymph node count. For Laura, surgery is 'doable'; she knows she will heal after the ordeal. We bring her home to our place until she is ready to be on her own. At night I lie with her in her childhood bed, looking out at the giant walnut trees swaying in the summer breeze.

"Mom, it should be you in this bed and me caring for you. This is all wrong."

Oh, if only I could take on her cancer. Is this not mother's love—to want to make life all better for her child? But all I can do is lie here, hold her in my arms, and feel my loving strength pour into her pain-filled body.

August 2, 2008

Laura packs her bags and returns to Hobbit House. Her delight in driving her own car again and no work for a week gives us reason to celebrate. She radiates health. With her daily arm exercises and longer walks, her strength returns. She calls us to say she can brush her hair with her elbow at shoulder level! Her determination demonstrates her resolve to thrive. Life almost feels normal again, until we go for another pathology report.

August 10, 2008

We wait in a tiny sealed-in room under brilliant florescent lights: we sit in orange plastic chairs; Laura sits on the examination table. Dr. J arrives. Laura stretches her arms out to him like a child drowning in deep water. He hugs her and he meets her eye to eye—her margins are not clear. The surrounding lymph nodes have cancer. Hearing the number, I realize they are the highest I have ever heard from any woman in the international workshops I have taught. Friends have died with lower numbers. A plug falls out of the base of my spine. Vital energy drains out of me. He explains to Laura the process of treatment--more surgery, time to heal followed by chemotherapy and radiation. As he starts to leave, Laura gets off the exam table to face him: "Before this next surgery I must make eye contact with you. I have to look into your eyes before I go under an anesthetic again." He promises. They hug. The secretary comes into the little room. She schedules new surgery dates for next week. Driving home we sit in numb silence. Laura asks to be dropped off at Hobbit House.

August 17, 2008

After 11 sobering hours at the hospital, Melissa moves into our home for the next 10 days. She takes over the kitchen, experimenting with new recipes that Laura can eat. She organizes her sister's huge cancer binder, putting the material in order for easy referencing during hospital appointments. Handyman-daddy-John goes to Hobbit House to complete outside jobs. I take on the roles of daily laundress, assistant cook, grocery shopper and hands-on–healer mom. Homecare nurses arrive, assuring Laura her stitches are healing. Laura's friends come to visit, bringing their youthful energy into our old home. Each evening, after watching a funny video, John reads to Laura until she falls asleep. It is a busy time and emotionally overwhelming, especially when Laura's pain level rises to "almost intolerable". Yet, we still find moments to celebrate the fullness of family living when loving laughter fills the old house. Neighbors and friends drop treats off at the door to help us endure this new and unknown territory.

The waiting time between each stage of Laura's treatments gives us space to take in the reality of cancer—surgery, waiting for pathology reports, pain control, side effects, chemotherapy drips, and radiation. Single words become two-week-long living realities where we fall into unknown territory. Love holds us together. We chew on these new experiences, digesting what we must. Tibetan prayer flags, a gift from a special friend, hang across our front porch like party flags waving in the winds. They catch prayers from our beloved friends and send our gratitude back to the world. We sense new energies surrounding us. Gratitude for the loving support brings us moments of peace. Though it is Laura's challenge to be the patient, it is our challenge to be flexible and gentle with each other. Respectfully, we listen to Laura's researched decisions, even when they petrify us. Island time provides John and me with a needed space for breathing more deeply and uncovers a clear, openhearted place to accept Laura's difficult choices.

Digesting the information affects us differently: Laura feels her body has betrayed and deceived her; Melissa assures us we are in this cancer journey together; John and I are numb. The mind and the heart do not know how to take in the reality of what is happening to darling Laura. Watching her, in the prime of her life experiencing cutting surgery, poisoning-chemo, and burning-radiation challenges us on all levels; yet she must endure them.

Laura decides to go back to her job at the university. Her colleagues create fun jobs that require her skills as a photographer and Photoshop expert. She walks in a curious landscape, going to work while living with a disease that threatens her life. She is determined to go to New York to complete her accreditation for Leadership Training. Chemo treatments will begin early September.

Before leaving for Colenso, I call my dear friend Margaret.

"Are you free for a visit?"

"Sure, come to the backyard. We can sit in the shade of the old walnut tree."

Sitting opposite her, I sob my heart out. "Oh Margaret, I just want to die into the void. I don't know if I can bear the weight of her dying. I fear I am losing my mind like a chipmunk, stunned by a fox. It shakes the poor thing to partial death. I am running in frantic circles of suffering. Will I collapse into insanity and tremble into madness? Will my flesh body be able to sustain this grief?"

She sits quietly, listening without comment. In silent moments, when I catch my breath, she mirrors key phrases back to me. "These are your words, Mary." I begin to hear my inner voice mirrored back to me.

"With the loss of hope, my soul dies. Despair becomes the enemy of my life. I am sinking into the darkness, Margaret."

"Can you describe what is there?"

"Velvet blackness…there are pin-prick holes where light shines through... where stars are born. I am descending into this hole. It is a portal into white light. A thread of light catches me. It is spinning me around and around but now stops, so I am facing the world. I see the living forms on our planet. I am overwhelmed with a Love for all that lives there. From earth we see stars in the midnight northern sky: from here I am star-light loving earth."

"Mary, can you hear this?"

"Oh Margaret, I am stunned like the chipmunk held in the teeth of a fox, but I only experience love— love for it, for the fox, for me, and oh, Margaret, I feel such gratitude for you in my life."

We hug goodbye through our tears. I am very aware that 26 years ago, Margaret had the same kind of cancer as Laura.

Before going back up north, I dream:

A caveman riding his Harley motorcycle finds me. I can't tell if he is Buddha or Christ. "There you are. I finally found you. Everything IS. LIVE IT!"

Melissa returns to the island with us for her final week of holidays. We have wonderful paddles in our kayaks. She and Laura talk daily on the phone. I hear the despair in Laura's voice when I pick up the call. Melissa's positive offerings balance my emotional turmoil. Yet, mother-flesh can't separate me from my beloved daughters. My physical heart knows this; my womb-heart lives this. Have I ever faced what death really is? When motherlove implants itself this deeply in the flesh, how can the pain of living the loss ever go away?

How can I accompany Laura if I project my fear of dying onto her? Maybe I fear ego death. An inner voice tells me that if I enter death's reality, my fear will make me crazy like a wounded chipmunk. Yet, I long for death, the fantasy that circles in my head of escaping into eternal peace. Must I experience psychological death, the end of the storyline I repeat to myself that sustains my sense of self? Meditating, I sense I am a black hole—nothing—no personality, no value. Focusing on my breath, attention drops deeper into subtle realities. An awareness of something hums throughout the black space of the hole. Another sensory awareness becomes apparent: instantly I recognize a state of existence that feels substantial, a Love that exists prior to the stories of me. A thought arises like vapor: I am a knotted core of light: the nothingness of light and the some-thingness-of form. My flesh knows that motherlove is a thread of this core light. I, as ego, can't change this.

Later, when I am with Laura, I feel a deep love for the wise soul she is. She lives her destiny with courage. As mother, I have the privilege to walk beside her. I recognize her individuality, her beauty as she travels through these darkening passages. My adult-self now dwells in a deeper awareness capable of loving her as she is: my frightened child-self feels too full of her own suffering to see anyone else. In the realm of sensate experience, I start to discern an energetic subtle difference— emotional turmoil feels like wind fluctuations in a storm, tossing my ego-boat like a cork in the waves. Attending to the deeper awareness, there is a field of unconditioned sensations that apprehend the storms and doesn't get caught in them. It is a quietness that lives at the bottom of a lake or an ocean that sees through all the disturbances to the light above. The peace at the bottom bares the full weight of the storm's force and remains free of the disturbance.

The phone rings. It is Laura: "My bones and organs are all clear, Mom!"

John hears the message. I hang up. We collapse into each other's arms and weep. The tension of holding ourselves together for so long releases.

Perhaps stage 3 cancer brings some hope. Laura flies off to New York for her training and tells us that on her return she is going to camp for a week to be normal again and enjoy Tim's friends. Then her medical leave will start.

3

CHEMOTHERAPY

"…And something ignited in my soul,
fever or unremembered wings,
and I went my own way,
deciphering
that burning fire."

–Pablo Neruda

Fall 2008

We drive back to the city where Laura's friends hold a pre-chemo hair cutting: "The bald and the beautiful, the young and the breastless." John shaves his head to set the standard for baldness. Laura is furious; she doesn't want to go; she doesn't want to draw attention to herself. She yells, "Fuck cancer," as she walks down the street alone to the gathering. My heart can barely stand her suffering.

Her hair dressing friend brushes her long chestnut brown hair, makes a ponytail and cuts it off—another bundle of beautiful hair to donate to kids' cancer wigs. She quickly shapes Laura's curls into a striking new style. When finished, Laura greets each friend with presence. I find it painful to witness. They all love her. After, I drive north to a retreat center to teach a weeklong BodySoul Intensive with Marion Woodman and Ann Skinner. I can almost believe my life is normal again… until I return home.

Walking into the chemo clinic, panic hits Laura. She only sees bald, sick, and dying old people. She is out of place. The cacophony of beeping machines makes it impossible to relax and focus. A young nurse recognizes her, quickly leads her to a recliner in the far corner, and gently inserts the drip tube. Laura immediately plugs into her relaxation tape and closes her eyes. Tears roll down her youthful face. I go numb. Hours later we leave. She picks up her bag of anti-nausea drugs and the steroids, drugs she is instructed to take for the next two weeks. After two days of being in a mindless fog and her insides feeling like flashing neon lights, she stops taking the steroids. She is utterly exhausted and can't sleep. Drained and thick headed, the thought of food makes her nauseous. Nothing has any flavor. Nibbling on Kraft dinner that normally she won't eat, she thanks me: "I must eat to get my strength back, Mom."

A week later she asks to go to the island until her next drip in two weeks. She loves the wild beauty of September colors. With her new camera she takes photos for her next Roary book, *Lions Get Sick Too*. In the morning, we walk the island together. In the afternoon, she plays chess with John. Their laughter ripples throughout the cabin. Late in the afternoon, the chemo headache hits. She lies on the couch, silently still. In the evening we take her in the canoe for a sunset paddle. She sits in the middle on cushions, her camera in hand. The soothing sound of our paddles, moving through the water, calms all our hearts.

During her third week after the drip, the headaches disappear. She begins to play with new rhymes for her next book, incorporating all that she is learning about hospitals, drugs, procedures, side effects, fears, new hopes, and dreams. She starts eating again, continuously snacking on high-calorie food to bring her weight back up. We go for longer walks on the trails of nearby Crown islands.

Her hair begins to fall out in chunks. I see her from the kitchen window, standing on the shoreline rocks, pulling out handfuls of her hair. She tosses them into the air where the winds gently carry her locks. She watches them float away down the channel. John goes out and holds her tightly in his arms as she cries. Such love. Such agony. On our last night she asks to be alone on the island. We leave in the boat to visit my cousins. Helping us get out of the boat, they take John in their arms and cry. Too painful to witness, I turn and look down the channel. The small shoreline maples are turning brilliant red in the cool September nights. I breathe in the color red. I trust the life-death-rebirth cycle of nature. This too shall pass creating space for next spring's blooming… breathe in 2, 3, 4… exhale out 2, 3, 4.

On our return to the city, Laura meets with her new oncologist, a bright young woman with long blond hair and about Laura's age. The doctor sits on the examination table swinging her long legs that end in red stiletto heels. In stark contrast, Laura is instructed to sit in a plastic chair beside us, her bald head revealing her perfectly shaped skull. She wears her beige Birkenstock sandals, old jeans and a green camp hoodie. Intellectually they are matched; their skills and knowledge base very different. Laura trusts her scientific knowledge and tolerates her difference in values. She names her new doctor, Dr. Stiletto.

The second chemo brings more side effects. The steroids before the drip day create flashing neon lights in her brain. She can't sleep; she can't concentrate. Chemo brain kicks in; it dumbs her down. On her computer she can't find the rhyming words or the pictures she took at the island. By the end of the second week, she starts to feel like herself again. Thanksgiving weekend, Melissa stays with Laura at Hobbit House. In the warm afternoons we take family walks in nearby woodland parks. Melissa's upbeat nature energizes Laura. They return to being kids again and with spirited laughter blow milkweed seeds out from their crispy pods. That night we share our traditional Thanksgiving turkey dinner with friends whose daughters are the same age.

The next day Melissa takes her for drip number three. They return to Hobbit House together. Since being told that she must take the steroids for two days after the drip to prevent heart failure, she obeys, but only for two days. Her mind goes numb; her eyes are heavy, her vision blurry and her balance wonky. These symptoms clear once she stops the steroids; but then she experiences depression from drug withdrawal. She wants to die. We begin to understand Dr. Stiletto's comment about taking Laura "to the point of death to kill the cancer and then I'll bring you back to life". Frustration erodes her spirits as she tries to weave these themes into her book, *Lions Get Sick Too*. Her creativity has always been a lifeline to her joy.

We spend a soul-killing day at the clinic when new liver scans are required. Laura unexpectedly finds she is a lesson for medical students. Speaking in technical terms, they discuss what they see on their screens as if she isn't there. She asks questions about the terminology they use. No one listens to her. Thinking she is dying, she cries. "Your family doctor will be sent all the information." No one offers her a Kleenex to dry her tears. Is this how doctors are trained? Insensitive bastards! Like a wild animal in pain Laura runs out of the hospital and without looking for cars, races through traffic to her home. John runs to get our car.

Outside the hospital I hear a madwoman yelling to the gods: "Fuck man's inhumanity to man. Fuck cancer. Fuck those cruel doctor bastards! Fuck! Fuck!" A male voice behind me gently asks if

I am OK. I suddenly realize I am the madwoman, out of my mind with rage and grief. I see our car with John driving towards me. I jump in. I am shaking like a dying leaf clinging to a barren branch. I call our compassionate family doctor and explain what happened. She listens and hears my plea for Laura. She respects Laura. That night she calls her at Hobbit House; her scans are clear! Who is insane—me or the medical 'healers' with their machines and iced-in hearts?

Though it is tempting to go numb, fall into fear, and deny the reality, I gradually learn to digest each day with more patience. In moments I feel gratitude for being together as a family. Our normal winter life starts to unfold. Laura remains independent except for appointments when we drive her to the clinic. John curls daily and works with immigrant families; Melissa returns to Toronto and to her high school students; I go to yoga and art classes and connect with dear friends. Before leaving for 10 days to teach a BodySoul Rhythms workshop in England, I book a series of alternative treatments for Laura—cranial sacral, massage, homeopathy, and lymph drainage. She joins classes at Wellspring, the support clinic for cancer patients and their families in London.

In Devon, England at the retreat center, I walk alone at sunrise on the moors. The sheep and wild ponies lift their heads above the gorse and look at me. I greet them respectfully. Nature nourishes my soul. I teach with more presence than usual. I find myself laughing and dancing freely as I lead the body warm-ups. In the company of like-minded, soulful women interested in the body-soul connection, I sense knots of physical tension in my gut loosen their grip. I am not a crazy lady; I am a mother living with the knowledge that cancer might kill her youngest daughter. Will I uncover a love big enough to embrace Laura in the here and the now and the eternal? Is this idealistic, or necessary for me to stay functional?

Chemo drip number four almost kills Laura. I hear Dr. Stiletto's words: "I take my patients almost to their deaths and I bring them back". What inflation!

Two days after the drip-day, Laura rests on our living room sofa. I watch life energy slowly drain out of her. She hasn't slept in two nights due to continual pins and needles in her hands and feet, a sign of nerve damage. Nausea, vomiting, and extreme pain in all her joints appear and she vomits all the anti-nausea pills. Then she can't swallow. The chemo causes a painful fungus to grow in her mouth, down her throat, and into the lining of the stomach. Dr. Stiletto never mentioned these side effects. At 4:00 am, John phones the cancer hospital emergency number; more pills are prescribed plus a numbing mouth wash. She now has 18 different pills. Trying to figure them out is exhausting for us. Despite this, John still has his sense of humor. Arriving home with more drugs he starts to laugh: "Who are we? Our daughter is curled up into the fetal position on the kitchen rug waiting for a soft-boiled egg to cook. My wife lives all day in her nightgown. I go out in a pink "fuck cancer" hat that keeps my shaved head warm. I bring home more drugs to add to our already drug-filled kitchen. Between the barf bowls and pill bottles in every room, what is this life we are living? Perhaps we need more prayers for the return of some semblance of normalcy." Lifting her head up from the rug, she looks at her dad through drug-glazed eyes. She smiles: "I just want to feel like myself again, Dad."

Later, I watch her life energy diminish. She is really sick. Every time I call the emergency cancer clinic the intern tells me that if her temperature is under 100 F, she is ok. But I know she is dying!

She has no vital energy. John calls our neighbor, a doctor at the cancer clinic. He runs across the street, takes one look at Laura and tells us to get in the car immediately. "Go to emergency... Now!" He calls the hospital for a bed. On our arrival at the emergency entrance, before she is even in her hospital room, she is hooked up to IV filled with antibiotics. By now her temperature is soaring; her immune system has turned against her. She is dying! I am impressed by the speed of action the minute she arrives. A lung X-ray and body scan are ordered along with tests for all her bodily fluids. John and I are asked to leave.

The next morning our neighbor visits her on his morning hospital rounds. He affirms she is in the right place, and just in time. John and I cancel our plans to go to Toronto. In a few days her vitality returns and along with it, her playful writing of rhymes for Roary's next book. She wants to do hospital photos for the book. I find two children's wheelchairs at the hospital entrance and take them to her room. John brings her camera and her stuffed characters, Roary and his lion friend, David Parker, "who lost his mane through some disease". I go down to the children's ward and find two little hospital gowns. Hearing Laura's laughter as she stages Roary and David's hospital pictures creates ripples of joy in our hearts. Our darling Laura is back! She is alive!

Four days in the hospital with more drugs pumped into her thin body, Laura's blood count returns to normal. She no longer remains severely dehydrated from all the vomiting. Apparently, an infection, caused by abscessing throat sores, was the problem. Through these hospital challenges, the value of being a family is a precious jewel. It is painful to watch a child endure the ordeals of life. We feel the pain of other families with loved ones in the hospital and simultaneously sense a love embracing us all. In the immediacy of extreme emotional suffering, I sense subtle warmth circulating throughout my body, calming me from the inside.

Before we leave the hospital, a $3,000.00 experimental drug is offered to prevent another occurrence. Fortunately, Laura's University Health Plan covers it. Her immune system will then be strong enough to endure the remaining chemo drips, but the side effects are nausea and joint pain. I am grateful for the privilege she has that gives her access to these drugs. I am disturbed that most patients do not have the same access. Without our neighbor's help, Laura may have died, like the young mother who had worked for Laura. She suddenly died during her third chemotherapy drip. She had stage 2 cancer: Laura's cancer is stage 3. What killed her—cancer or chemo?

December 8th, and chemo drip five flows smoothly. When her Toronto friends come to visit her at our home, I clean Hobbit House and John shovels the snow. We launder her towels and sheets and fill her kitchen with food she loves. She is eager to be strong enough to return to her independent living. She takes 20 different pills, staggered throughout the day. Pain killers help her to endure the joint pain. The side effects of the accumulated chemo destroy the lining in her throat and stomach, making it painful to eat. New cells won't grow until she finishes the treatments. Being her true warrior self, she expresses gratitude for any gesture of help and rarely complains. I feel it is all madness—drugs to kill the cancer, drugs to manage the cancer drugs, more drugs to manage the side effects of all the drugs! Someone is making a great deal of money out of this chemo-cancer business!

Once in her own home, Laura feels more herself. When she calls, I hear hope, joy, and laughter in her voice. Her beloved friends continue to visit her daily, supporting her, keeping her in contact with life beyond cancer. Looking forward to the end of chemo, she starts researching alternative treatments and natural remedies. She wants therapists who know her, who see her as a healthy young woman. For the last month at the cancer clinic she has seen different doctors and, though most were lovely, well-meaning people, they see her as 'breast cancer patient with chart # 20843'. Though her well-honed communication skills engage everyone at the clinic, it is hard for her to decide with strangers, who all *think* they can save her, what treatment options will keep her alive. She intuits that many doctors are terrified of cancer and dying. They are at war with cancer. Each one is convinced that their specialty will "kill the cancer," whereas Laura senses "living with cancer" is a more realistic option.

Christmas falls two weeks after chemo-drip five, the week Laura usually feels well again. She wears lovely hats on her bald head that her friends knit for her.

With earrings, penciled eyebrows, and translucent white chemo skin, she looks angelic. Steve, her new partner, makes her smile radiantly.

December: the season of darkness when the lights come on at 4:00 pm, I light candles throughout the house. I envision a turning point when new light appears on the horizon. I continue meditation practices to open into the silence of being. I sense the fragile nature of my personal life dancing within the infinite possibly of a shared human condition— love and loss, hope and despair. I hope the return of light will help me tenderly accept the reality I am living. Stepping into the year 2009, I also hope that our collective consciousness, seemingly determined to self-annihilate through raping earth's resources, will wake up to face the human shadow of greed and hording.

On Christmas Day we share our love and gratitude for dear friends and the abundance we live with. On December 29th, Laura welcomes her last chemo, number six. A shunt is inserted into her upper chest to handle the chemo as her veins have become too brittle to accept it. With her strengthened immune system, the side effects are greatly reduced. Melissa sits with her in the drip room, making Laura laugh as they remember their childhood experiences. We call the hospital days our family picnic time.

This time, when she starts to feel better in her third week after the drip, she knows she will continue to recover—diagnosis, treatment, recovery, LIFE!

4

RECOVERY

Don't run away from grief, o' soul
Look for the remedy inside the pain
because the rose came from the thorn
and the ruby came from a stone.

–Rumi

Winter 2009

In late February, after her post-treatment checkup, Laura flies to Florida to attend a 21-day retreat. Her days include lectures on the benefits of a living plant diet and detox treatments, private and group counseling, massage, cranial-sacral therapy, yoga, and meditation classes. She has time to dream new dreams in the sunshine by the pool.

With time at home, John starts curling again and helping his refugee families. I resume my international teaching with Marion and Ann. When home, I study watercolor painting and join an Inquiry group with

Diamond Heart practitioners. My boundaries expand outwards compelling me to question everything I experience. Unfamiliar impulses press into my body-space. My spiritual practice of finding words for deeply felt sensations helps to hone discernment skills. What new bulb, deep within my belly, sprouts roots that earth down into swamplands while extending upwards into sky space? The hope-despair pendulum continually challenges me. Sensing a new midpoint through sustained attention feels like uncovering new areas of awareness.

Editing my manuscript, *The Dragonfly Principle, An Exploration of the Body's Function in Unfolding Spirituality*, along with teaching, helps me maintain psychological balance. However, the underlying river of motherlove and fear continually flow through my fragile heart. I sense an inherent instinctual pattern of motherlove that is even more immense than my personal desire to have, hold, and love my own children.

When Laura returns home from the retreat, her enthusiasm for life is infectious. She looks wonderful, feels energetic and her creative juices are back. The upstairs sunroom in Hobbit House transforms into a grow-op for all sorts of sprouts. She informs the police that her home is not a marijuana garden but fresh living food for her to eat. Everything she plants grows wildly with her love for all living things. She shares the abundance of her harvest of living food with friends and family.

During one of our family Sunday dinners, Laura shares that she is never lonely. She questions herself if it is because she knows her beloved Tim never abandoned her when he died. I realize the gift she is giving us: her presence can never leave us. Real Love does that. She is also aware of the endless sorrow Tim's parents and sister have endured since his death. We too may face this. Is she preparing us for her death? Living with the unthinkable, I conceptually know I can't fight for her life. I can't run away either. I can't pretend my sleepless nights don't exist. Laura's chances of survival are slim. Thank heavens for marijuana to help me sleep. As our doctor affirms, it is better than any sleeping pill she could prescribe.

Anger is curious. When I rage at cancer for ruining her life and feel anger towards Tim for falling off a mountain and annihilating their planned future, I feel strong in my body and mind; but it doesn't last. Despair soon follows and touches into my sense of hopelessness. I can only be in the moment and accept what I cannot change. But words never touch raw emotions. A friend encourages me to publish some of the material in my group emails to the BodySoul leadership community. She claims my words are truthful and directly demonstrate the value of facing death, rather than pretending the situation will go away, if ignored. During cranial-sacral therapy sessions, I touch into the open moment where deeper truths, beyond my personal drama, are uncovered, exposed and revealed. An ancient voice speaks in my heart: "No birth; no death; birth yes; live curiosity." I feel Laura's presence in the room. A pain in my thorax feels as if I am having a heart attack. Light pours out of me, revealing a huge presence. Mine? Laura's? Presence in a unifying field? I write for clarity about the energetic, living experience of splitting open, of dying into light, into LIFE. If the unthinkable happens, will this bearable light of being live me?

Summer-Fall 2009

Though cold and wet, island time brings us hope. Laura calls in late May: mammogram and MRI are clear along with her bone scans. On hearing the news John and I hold each other tightly and cry out our fears of her dying. Maybe Laura will live. Maybe there is hope. In the fall we return to the city and share a fabulous weekend with both daughters. Melissa loves teaching high school dance and English courses in Toronto. She starts a vigorous Yoga teaching training course. Laura returns to her university job and rediscovers her gift of public speaking. John spends more time helping his Burmese families and other new arrivals to the city. He loves being with them, and they adore his warm, easy manner that penetrates through the language barrier. With our spirits positive, we enter the year's end of celebrations with uplifting thoughts and dreams of a future with two daughters.

I am immensely grateful for the BodySoul Community, a powerful international network for personal, collective and global facilitators. They are a faithful group of professional women committed to the inner workings of the soul and the outer expression of it through their honed skills as leaders. Their messages of feminine wisdom, both practical and divine, carry me through my darkest hours.

For two years we live in the cancer-free zone. When the YMCA director approaches Laura to join his management team, she leaves the university; but, only after a group medical plan agrees to cover her as a young woman with a history of cancer.

She found teaching new government legislation to 'old white, male professors' frustrating. They didn't want to learn. One tenured professor insisted that the university was just fine until she, like the other 'young know-it-all women', started taking over.

Laura joins the Y's management team as Vice President of Youth Engagement. The new job gives her a place to express her passion and expertise in delivering material she created for youth; programs concerning skill development, health and social issues. As a resource person for all departments and staff involving youth programs throughout the Y, Laura develops new models for local and international youth services. Her position demands she travel between cities—Baby Red, her first car, is traded in for classy Lady Red, a safe car for winter, highway driving.

Filled with hope for a future, Laura commits to 'Steve the architect', a caring older man with teenage sons. Knowing she can never have children, she felt it unfair to commit to a person her own age. During her early morning walks to the Y, she had noticed him in the coffee shop, smiling at her. Curious about his work, she introduced herself and their friendship began. Melissa also begins a new relationship with Erich, an English teacher at her school. Our life feels normal again.

5

SECOND ROUND

"…if we have divine love in our souls, no matter where we go we shall meet again."

–Paramahansa Yogananada

August 2010

Laura calls us at the island in tears. The cancer is back. We return home immediately. Surgery dates are set for mid-August while more scans are ordered.

Hope arises when we hear her bones are still clear; despair pushes in close behind.

Melissa leaves for India to study yoga at various retreat centers and ashrams.

Following Laura's third surgery, equally challenging as the two before, she stays with us until able to return to her Hobbit House. Mid-September she returns to work. With Steve in her daily life now, John and I fly to Chartres in France. We join Lauren

Artress and her French team to teach a Labyrinth workshop at the Cathedral. In the evenings, we rejoice with new international friends over delicious French food and wine. After the workshop, we take a train to Paris and celebrate our 40th wedding anniversary. For a week we play as we did on our honeymoon, savoring every minute as a carefree couple.

September 2010

On our return, Laura asks us to go with her to the cancer clinic, where she again meets Dr. Stiletto, the blond-haired, bright and beautiful oncologist. Again, she sits on the exam table swinging her exposed legs that end in expensive, black stiletto heels. Again, though without us in the room, Laura is assigned the lower white plastic chair. Dr. Stiletto suggests another round of chemo; Laura hesitates and asks more questions. Dr. Stiletto, looking down at Laura from her height, suggests Laura be a "good girl and do what the experts say because they know". In silent fury, Laura announces that the interview with her is over and walks out. In the car driving her to Hobbit House, Laura announces: Dr. Stiletto is fired. We agree.

Later, the cancer clinic calls to schedule an appointment with a radiologist. This doctor is very short and rather full of himself. Laura asks questions based on her research about the statistics for her age group: there are none; all studies are based on menopausal and post-menopausal women. Finally, he says; "You worry too much about the table setting when the Titanic is sinking". Laura quietly takes in his words. She calls Melissa to process her new reality, referring to her radiologist as "Dr. Half-a-Man". She agrees to do the radiation, as he suggests. Oh, how I love Laura's humor and courage! Oh, how I love Melissa's insights and the easy way she is with Laura!

In meditation I again face the question: Am I able to love Laura enough to watch her suffer more? Will my deep unconscious fear of her dying overwhelm me and contaminate her process? An ancient one whispers; "When you look outwards, see from deep inside yourself. Hear the music on both sides. Know you are the nexus." What is the music? The nexus? Inquiring into this non-conceptual, sensate landscape, I sense its unteachable nature. Only by living in that spaciousness will I know it, because I am it. Spaciousness emanates healing qualities, but if I become too immersed in it and identify with it, I am annihilated. When I ignore spaciousness, I drown in personal suffering.

I realize *thinking* about life radically differs from experiencing the dynamics of life, of existence. When I think, I detach from my body and live in my head. When I focus on body sensations, I connect to living flesh and a direct way of knowing. If I am to uncover something new from my experience of sensate motherlove, I must attend to what is present right now without translating the experience into familiar concepts. What is a woman's *real* capacity to love her child without identifying with the archetypal and instinctual power of motherlove?

Breathing in, I am full: breathing out, I am empty. Is this the full-empty pulse in all creation, like day and night, birth and death? Does the dance of life flow effortlessly into death, into nothingness? Is there a reverse flow of LIFE, a return to source, and then a turnaround into renewed outflow back into life? Is death dancing me into a void? Who is dying?

I can change nothing; yet, can I accept what is now? Meditating, I experience love melting the boundaries around personal likes and dislikes, judgements and learned ideas.

Laura starts another leave of absence, this time from the Y. Daily she walks to the cancer clinic for radiation treatments. On sunny days she invites friends or Steve to join her. If a colleague needs her professional input, she invites them to walk with her. Melissa comes home whenever she can. Together they look like young, happy sisters stepping into responsible adulthood. Laura devours the few cancer books by authors her age. Her curiosity inspires us; her courage and love for life permeates our space.

Meanwhile, I dream only of single images: a new house, a beach, a threshold, my stone collection. In one, I shop in a super store, but don't know what to look for; in another I discover original ways to dance that I didn't think were possible. I value the intimacy and safety of the Inquiry group I am part of with other Diamond Heart practitioners. We explore our inner landscapes and bring our shadows, both dark and light, into daily life. My heart is held in tenderness as I delve into the depths of darkness.

At the intensive BodySoul Rhythms workshop we study the psychology of the Demeter myth. I find myself relating to Demeter's rage when her daughter

Persephone is stolen and taken to the underworld with Hades. I sense my wrath that wants the whole world to be a scorched landscape like mine. I want everyone to feel my pain, my mother-suffering, my grief. A woman psychiatrist I knew, who died of cancer after a 20-year remission, visits me in a dream:

She whispers in my right ear: "I am right here, Mary. Death is not real: it IS the reality of LIFE. Be me. Live me. Know me. I will always be here, now. I have always been here. We are expressions of LOVE, sunbeams clothed in a human form. Our limited self-perception can't know the vastness that I AM. Expand into the vastness while tethered to the plexus, free of the illusion of a separate-suffering self. You are a tiny point of conscious emptiness in eternal space. Let that space speak in its language from that space."

Back in the workshop room, I witness my brain fog over. Like Demeter's wrath, my mother's rage at cancer eating my beloved Laura overwhelms me. Breathe…

A friend who is dying of the same kind of breast cancer as Laura calls me from the West Coast. Her oncologist suggests marijuana oil for depression, weight loss and insomnia as a more effective way to deal with symptoms. Drugs have side effects; weed has none. She suggests Laura try it. Laura smokes the odd joint; we all do, but where to find enough illegal buds in Ontario to make oil? After a long secretive search, I find enough weed to make it. With the help of a scientist friend, I make it on the front porch so I don't blow up the kitchen!

November 2010

I need to stay open to new possibilities and not sink into despair. When Laura comes for dinner, she exudes a maturity beyond her years. Her gratitude for her life rises like the sun each morning to celebrate a new day. I am an outworn husk. I am the one dying, the one sinking into dark earth, spiraling down to rot in winter. Yet, like Laura, I am curious about life: I inquire into the feeling of being pulled downward towards composting darkness, annihilation of self, of death. In stillness, attention travels in unknown fields towards a distant horizon of felt chaos. Do I dare continue and peek over the edge of that threshold? Where is my survival instinct? My sense of being myself isn't down here. I have no sense of a self. I feel no mother-grief! I exist. I am awareness, cloaked in an atmosphere of sad love.

Melissa arrives home for the Christmas break to be with Laura. Oh, how I love those two faces peering through the front door window—such joy, such beauty, such youth! Full of laughter, they trim the living, naked Christmas tree with all the funny ornaments they collected as children. They put the ugliest ones they made in the front. Their favorite children's Christmas music plays as they dance around the tree recounting disastrous family outings that now seem hilarious. Christmas Eve, we walk in the city park under twinkling lights as we have done for years. They decide to sleep in their children's beds to see if Santa still comes to our old home.

Christmas morning Laura puts the coffee on and wakes us all up. Their stockings are full to the brim with feminine items and organic household cleaning products. They express endless gratitude for our parenting over the years, our generosity, and our love. After the usual Christmas breakfast of coffee cake, we walk in our favorite woods. The deep gullied ponds where we once skated are frozen solid.

They return to Hobbit House: Laura to phone her beloved Tim's family; Melissa to reconnect with Erich and friends. We enjoy our annual Christmas dinner with dear friends. The four adult daughters share stories, careers, loves and interests. They have matured. We marvel at their capacity for intelligent conversation, so different from the quiet little girls of the past. Driving them back to Hobbit House, we all agree it has been a wonderful Christmas.

As we drive home, John joyfully recounts the highlights of the evening. Looking into the cold darkness of winter's night, two wishful futures appear—Laura free of cancer, in love and vitally involved with her job; Melissa married with two little kids. The coin flips—Melissa alone in Toronto and Laura slowly dying in Hobbit House.

Breath leaves me; I freeze my mind and go numb.

6

ROUND THREE

"By being with yourself…by watching yourself in your daily life…with the intention to understand rather than to judge, in full acceptance of whatever may emerge, because it is there, you encourage the deep to come to the surface and enrich your life."

–Nisargadatta Mahara, *I Am That*

January 2011

Laura finds another lump in her breast. More tests are immediately scheduled. The cancer has returned with renewed energy. She asks we do not call her. After a week of silence, the phone rings. She can no longer deny her situation; Dr. Half-a-man is right; the ship is going down; Tamoxifen is not working. She returns to the dreaded cancer clinic and courageously surrenders to the doctor's advice. To stay alive, she must leave her beloved job, hire a replacement, go on long-term disability, have more surgery, complete another 6 months of chemo followed up with more radiation. She calls Steve to take her home.

In despair, John and I continue the trajectory of our own lives: he returns to curling and helping refugees while I fly to Chicago to teach. In February we blindly walk with Laura through hospital halls to meet her new female surgeon, her new oncologist, and her radiologist. In silence we witness Laura ask detailed questions to her surgeon. With her communication skills, she knows how to create an open dialogue free of negativity. Her engaging presence warms the atmosphere. The oncologist suggests she try a new experimental drug: the perk will be free massages and manicures. Dr. Half-a-man claims he will cure her with his radiation.

To sleep at night, I start smoking marijuana again to quell my fear. John watches sports on TV late into the night. Early in the morning I find him downstairs reading the newspaper. In the evening we walk the neighborhood holding hands like a pair of lovers afraid of losing one another in the storm. We lose weight; our voices drop; our faces age with strain.

After her surgery, we care for Laura at home. Once strong enough, she later returns to Hobbit House for what is left of her life. She needs Steve and her friends. We decide to fly to New York with my cousins for an extended weekend of theatre and art galleries. We need to laugh, to join the human race and prepare for what lies ahead.

Meditating at home, I focus on a sensation of volume in my body, the inner space where impulses, feelings and thoughts arise. In my solar plexus, fear, hope and despair swirl around like roller coaster rides. Deep in my belly I discern a silent core— dark, weighted and absorptive. In my thorax, I sense energy that is light, buoyant and joyful. How I feel depends on where I place attention. At the Inquiry group, I focus on different sensations, each presenting a unique feeling with accompanying voices. Under the noise, I uncover sensations free of thought. They just are—everything exists in harmony. When I place my attention on my heart, an elusive sense of rose perfume arises up through my neck. Like vapor, it permeates through the invisible space within.

Love permeates all that I am.

That night I dream:

I am in a huge ancient church with many rooms. Dancing through them I am to explore each one. I don't have a clue where to go or what dance steps are needed. I understand I am to improvise without any preconceived ideas about what dancing really is.

I wake up remembering Laura starts her 30 consecutive days of radiation. Grief swells inside me.

Again, Laura walks daily to her radiation treatment with friends and colleagues. When her senior mentors call to process something at work, she invites them to accompany her. She seems to welcome others into a safe space where they can share their burdens. She never shares what they say but marvels at human complexity.

Laura's skin starts to blister despite the hospital's preventative cream. It burns even with ice packs. I make more marijuana oil to help her sleep without pain while she orders a homeopathic cream for fourth-degree burns. Both work. I wonder if radiation will kill her before the cancer does. I dwell in the cave of fear. Meditating and drawing help me to focus elsewhere, bringing temporary relief.

We open the island mid-April to prepare for the summer, post radiation. The rocks feel solid, strong and silent; the wind in the pines lulls us to sleep; the water absorbs our attention as it constantly shifts patterns along the shoreline. We breathe deeper taking in pure, fresh air. Held by nature's spacious beauty, we spend our days clearing winter debris, pulling weeds, cleaning boats and cabins, all in preparation for summer's bloom.

After her final radiation treatment, I pick up Laura and drive to the marina. John follows us in Laura's car; she wants to be free to come and go. The Y has given her a new Blackberry phone; she playfully delights in her newest work toy, her laughter soothing my aching heart. By the time we arrive at the docks, she has mastered her toy. That night I dream:

> *John and I walk hand in hand to the shoreline*
> *where we watch a full moon rise. Aboriginals*
> *arrive in their birch bark canoe. They have been*
> *looking for us for a long time and are delighted to*
> *find us on Colenso. Hope flutters in my belly.*

Melissa and Steve arrive for an extra-long weekend to celebrate John's birthday followed by

Mother's Day and Father's Day. Late spring, Melissa leaves for her last month of teaching and Laura, returns to work. Early July, cousins arrive with their extended families to open up their own little islands. We celebrate being alive. The cabin fills with joy, love, expectations, and happiness. I breathe into each moment, fully aware that this too will pass. Staying in the present moment, I marvel at my great motherlove for our two adult daughters. John and I find ourselves walking in gratitude for our life, repeating 'thank you, thank you' to the trees, the sky, the water, the rocks, and the wildlife… and to each other.

The CEO at the Y asks Laura to be a director of something. She doesn't care about titles. She delights in his suggestion she be 'Director of Youth Leadership Training for Southwestern Ontario and International Development'. Joyfully she designs new programs, gives keynote speeches and engages youth leaders to speak in public about their experiences as a means to evaluate her programs. Repeatedly she expresses gratitude for her life, her education, her friends and all who have enabled her to fulfill her dream in this job.

During this time I live between three states of awareness: fear of Laura dying, resistance to change and an unknown darkness that attracts and frightens me. In my head I know fear arises from ego identification when I can't fix life the way I want. I also discern my reluctance to dig deeper. What will I uncover underneath my familiar sense of self? In meditation I detect a point of attention that perceives ego thinking as limiting and isolating within the familiar loops of my conditioning. Attention has a wider lens when I relax into subterranean and unfamiliar openness. Experiencing the widening, the ego-voice of fear threatens my sanity. Going beyond the words into felt sensation, I uncover I am part of an integrated field. It is warmed by an inner golden sun. Unfamiliar visions arise. In this space, I am a knower, dwelling inside spiritual qualities. I no longer think; I am thought. Something other is in charge. A dream follows the waking experience:

I am walking a space-labyrinth where a spaceship stabilizes the center. An old man takes notes as I speak of my experience. I am shocked he is interested;

for in my mind, I know nothing—my body simply performs the actions necessary to walk the labyrinth with its twists and turns and open spaces.

The dreams communicate to me to trust my instincts and know where the images are taking me. One night I dream:

I am wearing my life jacket as I explore an unknown, semi-dark room. I see a Chinese woman crying uncontrollably. I have met her somewhere before. In her grief she says, "Get down to the crustacean level where you will find flesh-colored powder of ground-up bones. It is now digestible."

Melissa speaks more and more about Erich. She brings him to the island where we realize they are deeply in love. We delight in their presence; they are committed and well-suited. Emotionally I am stretched between their happiness and Laura's lingering sorrow.

7

BREATHING SPACE

*"Within us is the soul of the whole, the wise silence,
the universal beauty, the eternal One."*

–Ralph Waldo Emerson

Fall 2011

Back in the city for winter, our life feels normal. Laura, recovered from radiation, appreciates the responsibility and creativity in her new job. Melissa is happily in love with Erich and enjoys teaching. John curls daily; I work out at the Y; we celebrate our retired life with friends. Even in my inner life, I sense an open space of relative calm. It demands my attention for I know it can flip any moment into despair and fear. I dream:

*A golden colored man emerges from an unknown lake
to warn me that an alligator is swimming towards
the shore. Instinctively I know not to corner it.
Communicating telepathically, he tells me: "Keep your*

attention on the alligator; treat it compassionately;
be not afraid, and give it lots of space."

Later, I dream:

An unknown woman appears. A golden thread, linked
to the sky, is connected into her neck. The thread is
being pulled out of her from above, but it keeps on
being pulled out. I fear the woman will unravel.

Working with these images, I know archetypes have negative and positive energy. Threats of annihilation from the alligator energy and spiritual guidance of the golden man and golden thread, both exist in me. I inquire into the sensations within each discrete image, feeling a midpoint existing between the *felt* energies of being pulled out of myself while being cautious of spiritual and physical annihilation. I am being pulled apart into opposite directions, up to spirit and down into physicality. Space is created between the two poles. Twisting threads of energy untangle and reweave to create an experience of being a luminous body in space. Perhaps something new wants to be realized, wants to be expressed in the world. My head feels like a midpoint existing between raw instinct below me and unconditioned spirit above me. To maintain a position sandwiched between me-centered survival and other-centered Life, between personal stability and impersonal forces beyond my control, requires the wisdom of a dancing self.

I write in my journal: "The alligator is unconscious instinct; the golden thread is unconscious spirit. Both require my attention. Perhaps a new capacity to experience another way of being is now possible if I awaken to these unconscious parts."

When dancing, I know experientially, the balance point between a stable core and ceaseless motion. Rigorous training and endless repetition—balancing through falls and recoveries, leaps with secure landings, ground rolls to standing with twists and leaping turns—develops sovereignty over physical expression. Eventually, a stable core allows me to open spontaneously to the creative impulses that continually transform energy in my body. In the dancing I am transformed; I am beauty in motion, reflecting waves of harmonic rhythms pulsating through my limbs. Without thought I trust my trained body to execute what spirit demands.

Attention transmutes into a silent knower embedded within a dancing self invisibly rooted in

Life. Do the images point me in the direction of field awareness, the expanding awareness of soul's dimension, both timeless and unbound? Does soul simultaneously discern uniqueness while synthesizing the parts into an experience of wholeness--presence? Is it presence that dances me uniquely into life? Or, will I unravel into a heap of disconnected threads? Is there an inborn capacity to leap into new unbound space? When did I sign up for this course—at birth or before? Who is the choreographer? What breathes me? Humbly, I accept I have no answers.

More dream images guide me. In one:

I give Laura two bracelets: one crystal the other red coral. She must decide which one to wear and when.

Both images reveal spirit illumining physical reality, red coral for physical life and crystal for spiritual insight. The other image is the great oak tree in the center of Colenso that we call Zeus. Its roots hold the rocks and soil of the island together, while its great branches stretch up into the sunlight above the cedars, giving shape to the entire island. In the dream:

Zeus says to me: "All things grow down, branch out, and reach up from a stable center."

Meditating, I feel a subtle guidance inside the images directing me into unknown, unconscious and unfamiliar depths.

Laura must choose her own path. I must uncover another center, one that grows in all directions. I begin to experience tic-toc time as a mental construct superimposed over a transparent field of timeless space. Like the dream of the labyrinth spaceship, the whole of terrestrial Life embraces other realties, animating physical life from within. Physical life consists of differing living substances and like earth, lives in an unbound cosmos. Is there a midpoint, a conjunction where unknown human potential is realized and new capacities emerge? Days of silence; I wait.

Winter 2012

Such a wonderful Christmas! Both daughters decide to stay home and share Christmas Eve and morning with us. Their homemade stockings are full to the brim. When Laura goes downstairs, she delights that Santa still comes down our chimney. Their playful bantering and obvious enjoyment in each other fills me with new hope, new joy and new expectation. A dream supports my hope while giving me guidance:

I am given a new car. I don't have a clue how to drive it. The instruction book reads; "Remember you are not the car, only the driver. This car is self-driving!

When teaching, I suddenly sense moments of insecurity when a cruel internal voice tells me I am a stupid woman and unworthy of life. A wave of panic grabs my solar plexus until deep breathing relaxes me. At night a dream threatens me. I do not know what I am doing. To compensate when teaching, I puff myself up with tension to feel like my confident know-it-all gifted teacher self. I am like my homemade soup with a base of frozen stock and leftover dying vegetables. What a mess! Living unconsciously in familiar habits and puffed up with ego self-importance is so much easier than waking up…or is it?

Meanwhile, Laura and Steve take a holiday to the Caribbean and Melissa and Erich move in together. One night I dream:

I make a new foot path through the swamp land behind Colenso that is no longer underwater. A large granite rock rolls into the center of this path. I am delighted to dance around it, leap off the top, land securely and roll about in laughing joy.

If only this were real! Maybe one day…

Over the holiday, Melissa and Erich move into Hobbit House to be with Laura and Steve. They are good friends and oh, how my heart beats with new joy when they come for dinner. A dream image lands me in reality:

It is a perfectly calm summer day. I stand at the edge of a high cliff and without knowing how, I carefully climb down towards the clear saltwater. I see an unfamiliar boat on the horizon. I put on my life jacket and swim towards it, not knowing how far away it is. I simply know in my bones it will pick me up.

On waking a voice tells me that the right music is essential for swimming long distances.

When dancing, I am music made visible. During my entire teaching career, I have listened to endless selections of music, feeling the ambiance created. I was born with an intelligence to feel music and recognize what is conducive to supporting soul qualities, and what supports egoic expressions. Many are puff-me-uppers and fun, while others support the natural beauty inside suffering.

John and I open the island early this year. As always, we are full of anticipation. Surprisingly, I fall flat on my belly when stepping onto the dock—aging?—a forewarning?—lack of attention? I ignore it, but it haunts me like that dream alligator. Now that I am a senior, I try to walk and kayak with more mindfulness. I meditate each morning, sketch and play with watercolors, pull out weeds in the garden and watch the wildlife. The healing atmosphere of living in and with nature uplifts me. I feel reassured that the natural world, though beautiful is also terrible—life forms eat life forms. I witness one animal digesting another to survive, plants absorbing earth nutrients and rays of sunlight. In these harmonically balanced rhythms, I exist. I know what nourishes me—fresh air, good food and wilderness; but what eats me? Am I a parasite or are humans designed especially for a unique and purposeful function?

One midsummer morning I wake up crying from a dream:

An ancient sage is building a new structure on Peak Island, the crown island beside us. The beams are solid pine logs he hued from the land. I explore his structure. When I stand in the living space, I have views in all directions. In the corner is a composting toilet like we have in the cabin. The sage pours liquid golden shit from a jar that his departed grandson left for him. I say to him, "You do this too?" He smiles knowingly.

I don't know what it means. I keep doing what I love to do. Watching the news, I grieve with mothers who hold their dying children in their arms; their sorrow bleeds into mine, my solar plexus echoing their pain. We become one: a field of subjective grief lived as a universal, objective fact. My awareness expands into a vaster field encircling all mothers. Our collective mother-body knows how to transform our flesh into a fetus. A discerning motherlove at this deeper reality of shared experience holds personal suffering, collective suffering and world sorrow. Silent tears dissolve the sense of boundaries between me and all mothers. Universal Oneness becomes real. Parents are not meant to bury their children; it reverses the archetype in the natural world—birth, life, death, compost, renewal. Something beyond keeps us breathing through all our suffering.

Summer 2012

Laura, Steve, Melissa, and Erich are with us for a week of summer holidays. On a perfect morning—

still water, no clouds, clear sky—Laura announces that we ought to seize the day, gather the extended family together in their boats and ride out to a distant cluster of shoals for a picnic. Days like this are rare when we can navigate a safe-water path through treacherous underwater rocks and shoals. While John teaches Steve and Erich how to sense the water's depth, I watch Laura and Melissa in the bow rider nattering away. Arriving is always challenging with anchors, ropes, deciding where to tie up with no dock and unloading people with food coolers on precarious rocky footing. The sense of celebration fills me with momentary joy… but will Laura be with us next year?

Sitting with my cousins on the shore, we watch the younger generation dive off the high rocks and swim in the crystal-clear waters around smooth pink-rock shoals. I love hearing their chattering laughter just as we, our parents and grandparents once did. We toast our ancestors, our Nana and Grandpa, who sought out the open waters of Georgian Bay. They built their clapboard cottage and with their five children and a cow swimming in tow, they rowed to their summer cabin on the rocks.

As we toast them, I feel the mother-line that brought me here to this moment in time. This is how I expected my life would be: a family of six with grandchildren yet to arrive. Back at the cottage, Laura and Melissa create a beautiful vegetarian meal; John and I clean up. I share a joint with the younger folks, who rarely drink alcohol but enjoy the playful effects of marijuana. Laura and I share a spirited conversation. I explain the symbol w/hole that I use to refer to the Oneness of Life (whole) and the reality of the hole if the ego disengages from it. It is the hole that lets the light in from the surrounding whole. Laura, laughing with approval says: "That's good mommy. I get it." Inside my heart whispers, "Oh how I will miss her." That night I dream:

> *I am in a workshop. I am demonstrating agony as a symbol in the body. Jiddu Krishnamurti, who witnesses me, says, "This woman knows agony."*

The next morning Melissa leaves early with Erich. When saying goodbye to her sister, Laura cries uncontrollably. I turn away and watch two loons fly high above us with their haunting cries. When Laura and Steve leave later in the day, they are subdued.

During dinner we silently watch two deer swim across the channel.

On the last weekend of summer, Laura and Steve return. Running down to the dock I catch a glimpse of Laura's greying field. My heart sinks: she is dying. Later, sitting on the rocks, our toes in the water, Laura cries beside me. "Oh mommy, I can't breathe deeply anymore. I get strange headaches. I know I am working too hard, but I love my job and my life so much. I don't want to die, Mom."

John continues to be plagued by a nagging infection; my sister with Alzheimer's comes to live with us on the island after her husband Carl cuts most of his thumb off and is too drugged on painkillers to care for her. I wonder if my center will hold. I feel like the plaster in a mosaic, holding the pieces of me in place, but disintegrating.

Keep breathing… hold her…my mother-voice sobs inside me. "Oh don't let her die." On her return home to London, Laura sees her beloved family doctor. Scans and tests are ordered.

After seeing the heart and lung specialist, Laura calls us on her 33rd Birthday: "He said it is stress related and I am to take a leave of absence". John and I fall into each other's arms and weep our tears of relief.

We wait two weeks for Dr. Half a Man's appointment. Recognizing the symptoms, he tells her immediately the cancer has spread into her brain. She asks us to stay at the island until the new tests have started. To stay sane, I make marijuana oil from this year's garden of four plants. Laura may need it for pain control. It is all I can do now to feel helpful. Steve, stable as always, carries the emotional load, living with her in London.

8

BACK IN THE TRENCHES

"Every daughter contains her mother in herself and every daughter her mother, and every woman extends backwards into her mother and forwards into her daughter."

–C. G. Jung

Fall 2012

A new level of despair seeps into our bones. We accompany Laura through three different hospitals where she undergoes mammograms, ultrasounds, biopsies and the MRI machine. I am aware that this month, eight years ago, her beloved Tim died. I taste her sadness; I hardly eat. I see the weight of grief in John's stooping shoulders. Steve grows more silent.

On a warm fall day, I meet Laura and Steve while vegetable shopping in the farmer's market. The night before they went to an auction house exploring for treasures. She looks happy as she reaches for her organic broccoli; Steve looks drained. We hug and part. At home, I receive news two women from the BodySoul community have died of breast cancer. Life and death, giving and receiving, transform into an unbroken flow of deep Love. Swirling through the bedrock of emotion I feel the timeless flow outside my experience of inner despair. The choppy emotional waters of mechanical tic toc time stagnate the eternal flow.

Thanksgiving weekend the extended family gathers at John's sisters. The young cousins, now with partners, bond instantly. Late into the night John hears Laura in the living room. She can't breathe lying down in bed. She curls into her daddy's arms on the living room couch where they spend the night sitting up. I take a sleeping pill, knowing that one of us must function to get us home. Steve takes the opportunity to sleep as well. Melissa lets us know that she has arranged for a leave of absence from teaching whenever we need her. I feel her love and strength, her loss and vulnerability. I love her dearly. Thank heavens she has Erich to support and love her.

When all the test results are in, our family doctor calls me. I am to gather our family together for a consultation in our home this afternoon.

There will be no surgery. Any intervention will be palliative. Laura sits on the couch and weeps, not taking in what palliative means for her. Dr. A arranges for a hospice team, assuring Laura that her time is not yet. The hospice team will accompany her from here on and in her own home.

We sit like stones; I go brain dead. Steve and Laura return to Hobbit House. John goes to the basement like a zombie to watch sports. That night I dream:

> *A gunshot explodes in the midnight sky. Petals of a white magnolia flower, released from their center stem, float effortlessly in a black void. I sense an unfamiliar deep peace and am touched by loving joy that defies my normal sense of self. The image simultaneously terrifies and comforts me.*

On waking I breathe in one of the floating petals, letting it come to rest in my heart.

At the cancer clinic the next day my robot body carries on as normal. Laura's hospice oncologist, Dr. H, tells her a different type of chemo will eat up the cancer in her lungs. This will not cure her; but it will help her breath with ease again. Laura loves her new oncologist, who sees her as an intelligent adult capable of understanding the treatments. We drive back with Laura to Hobbit House to clean her home. Laura, still breathing with difficulty, lovingly dusts each treasured object, found at auctions over the years. I vacuum. John works outside, completing the autumn chores to maintain her home over winter. Steve arrives after work with Laura's favorite takeout dinner. We leave with a pile of laundry.

To reclaim some sense of normalcy, I teach a seminar series in London with Marion and Ann. On the first night, I dream that a stranger gives me a large, jeweled ball held together by a golden thread. When I am away and Steve works, John helps Laura around her house. That night he shares with me that Laura's bone pain is increasing. New painful lymph nodes now grow on her spine. The doctor assures her these symptoms will disappear the following week after the first chemo drip.

The CEO at the Y, who Laura refers to as "boss man," calls her: "At the Y we are one family, Laura. This morning I sent a memo to all staff that when they are visiting you, they are working for the Y." This delights Laura. She loves her Y colleagues and needs their youthful energy. And, they need her 'out-of-the-box' problem-solving skills to help them carry on without her. She has much to live for: new

Roary books to write and photos to take to support the rhymes, young people to mentor, a loving relationship with Steve and many loving friends of all age who visit her regularly.

Melissa drives to London to accompany Laura for the first chemo drip. She makes Laura laugh as the cancer drinks up the poison. This time she doesn't fear the discomfort of the procedure. Before returning to Toronto, Melissa sets up a surprise sleepover at Hobbit House for the "Never Wives Club," a wonderful group of Laura's buddies who vow never to marry. Laura can hardly wait to see her gaggle of friends again.

Now that stage 4 cancer is confirmed, any treatments are directed to control symptoms and improve her quality of life. Dr. A., with her practical, realistic knowledge and compassionate heart, assures Laura that her symptoms will lessen in a few weeks. Her breathing will return to normal, and she will regain an appetite. Watching the dynamic between doctor and patient, I know we are blessed to be under the positive and intelligent care of a family doctor who does home visits. She treats Laura first and then, turns to support us as well. She also gives

Roary books to young parents with children who are dealing with a family member dying of cancer.

John looks pale and drained. The infection he had over the summer still plagues him. He drags his body through the days. In November, Laura feels her symptoms disappearing. The marijuana oil I made helps her sleep and gives her a bit of an appetite. There is lightness in her mood when she talks about her home becoming a Y center for her friends. Laughter fills her home during the day; Steve keeps her company at night. Laura breathes more easily after the treatment and her friends start to take her to chemo drips.

After the hospital 'drip-days' she stays with us to give Steve a break. These are rough nights. Steroids, necessary during chemo drips to prevent sudden heart failure, keep her wide awake at night. John stays up with her, watching old movies. I knock myself out with a sleeping pill to function the next day. Friends have us for dinner to keep our spirits up, but the ache in my heart never leaves. My solar plexus keeps turning like a Ferris wheel without controls.

Palliative radiation follows her weekly chemo drips. Dr. Half-a-man, looking at her brain scans tells her she must have brain radiation. Laura asks about the process and outcome. Listening, she realizes her life is unraveling: she will never be able to work again; she will lose her creativity; her hair will fall out again. He tells her there will be several treatments. The initial headaches from the radiation can be controlled by steroids. I demand he give her the prescription now. In the middle of night, to think we can phone the hospital and then go to a drugstore is cruel thinking. Reluctantly, he acquiesces.

"Is there any hope?" she asks, looking into his avoiding eyes.

"There is some. I do not want to give you a false impression. You are young; your heart is strong and will support you."

"Are we talking months? Years? Should I call my sister home?"

"It is wise to get your life together, to get things done in these next three months."

Steve comes with her for dinner. Picking at her meal, tears roll down her lovely face. Scared and frightened, she tells us she needs to spend the night alone.

Beautiful Laura is dying before our eyes in bits and pieces. How will my heart ever hold onto living? Not only am I losing Laura, but I am witnessing John's playful optimism slowly fade away. Melissa will lose her sister, her best and dearest friend. Somehow our 40 years of marriage contains our grief, embracing us in a mysterious field of deep loving silence. No matter how penetrating the grief, this field embraces us throughout our days, expands, grows more substantial and becomes tenderly textured. I begin to trust a growing awareness of light in the darkness, of the power of love inside the dying process.

When I feel I am passing out, I lie on the floor in the front room. Winter sunlight streams through the window. I listen to a meditation tape my yoga teacher made. Relaxing into the supporting floor, I feel myself slipping into sleep. On awakening I write in my journal:

When I perceive myself as a solid visible form, I am a mother grieving the slow death of her daughter. However, when I perceive myself as the invisible dancing light, I feel the need to be creative, to express what is inside me, to become conscious of the energy and then give it visible form. I notice that the inner light never clings to its outer form. It translates impulses of vital energy within the images into authentic self-expression in the outer visible world. This process of transforming impulses happens from birth to death; it is contained within the whole of Life. I sense the cosmos pulsating itself into being, into a world made manifest. Birth and death are beginnings and endings; a visible event emerging out of and returning to, the One invisible dynamic field of the LIFE of the cosmos.

I drop back into silence. An inner voice whispers: "I just want to die." It alarms me, yet it feels like a truth freshly uncovered. I look out at the darkening November day. I dislike cold, long, sunless days. Throughout the rhythm of the seasons something keeps breathing me even when I want to stop.

The phone rings. It is Melissa. She is crying.

"Laura says she is dying, Mom. She wants more time to heal herself. She wants another summer at the island, and I can't do anything to help her."

"Your love for your sister always makes her happy, Melissa. I know your loving connection with her helps her more than you can imagine. It seems like so little, but darling, it is so much. You are there for her. She trusts you, loves you. It is all we can do now."

John calls his sister with our difficult news. Their happy news is that their son is a new father of a baby boy. We face death; they celebrate a birth. John goes to the curling rink. My dear neighbor drives me silently to Aqua Fit, where she protects me from anyone approaching me to chatter. I am grateful and humbled by her silent empathic care for me.

Before taking Laura for the first brain radiation zap, John takes her to the bank manager. She knows she must sign over all her banking needs to him, including the ownership and mortgage payments of her beloved Hobbit House. John finds her transformed; she walks with confidence; she looks stunning. She is up and out and in charge of her life.

Walking into Dr. Half-a-Man's office she announces: "Your timeline for me is three months. I accept that. I am not in denial. I did my mortgage and called my out-of-town friends to come and say good-bye. But Dr., that is not my timeline. In eight months, I am going to the island to stay for five months. So, after full brain radiation treatment, what are your plans for me?"

Our darling Laura is back!

She weighs 105 pounds, 20 pounds less than her healthy camp days. Melissa takes time off teaching to live at Hobbit House and accompany Laura for her first full week of radiation zaps. The steroids for brain swelling make her crave food she never eats:

hamburgers, French fires, and sugar donuts. When Melissa walks with her around the block, Laura clings to her arm. Feeling spaced out; she fears falling and tires quickly. On her steroid days she tries to eat to gain weight. The marijuana oil helps her sleep deeply while increasing her appetite. At her last radiation she clings onto my arm for stability, like an elderly woman. I savor the warmth of her physical closeness and mourn that she needs my help to stand up now. The scene is all wrong. She ought to be supporting her aging mom.

On the day I lead a Labyrinth workshop for Wellspring, a clinic for families dealing with cancer, Laura's hair falls out again. I know I am one with the participants, all grieving souls. Walking together in silence, I feel the beauty of communion, so different from the advertising world that markets endless material stuff we don't need. I am thankful for the labyrinth that holds us in presence. That night I dream:

I am white light trying to figure out how to
mend the vibrant green ivy growing up inside
my spine as it stretches towards the sky.

Laura awakens with glassy-eyes and craving grilled cheese sandwiches that John has made for her.

She wants to go home later to meditate in her upstairs room with a south exposure and all her plants. Focusing is a challenge for her. New pus- filled hives appear on her belly. She imagines the puss filled with cancer pouring out of her radiated skin. Fortunately, antihistamines keep the itch under control.

With the intense days of brain radiation completed, she returns to the cancer clinic to meet her oncologist. Laura appreciates the doctor's openness, her upbeat conviction that she will help make Laura's life, whatever is left of it, livable and worthwhile. Laura re-starts the weekly palliative chemo drips that keep her breathing comfortably. This time the anti-nausea pills work, giving her a little appetite to maintain her thinning body.

On the weekend, Melissa and Erich stay with Laura and Steve. After a fun-filled dinner with both couples at our table, I plunge into despair. The thought of Steve and Laura not with us in the future seems impossible. I feel I am dumbing down. I rarely remember what I read. I am more sensitive to my own and other's suffering. I know I am depressed—the loss of soul and faded expectant hope. Physical exercise sustains us. The daily outing for Aqua Fit or yoga seems to keep my heart beating. John arrives home from curling with more energy than when he left.

Laura's friends continue to come to Hobbit House, bringing books and flowers, special food and new plants for her meditation room. The HR woman from the Y sits on her bed to help Laura fill out the long-term disability forms. My friends go to her home to give her massages, cranial sacral sessions and Reiki treatments. Always a close friend brings her dinner, and Steve faithfully comes right after work to be with her for the long dark evenings and scary nights. Through her morning meditation she re-composes herself, greets her friends and receives their caring love. For now, this sustains her. We remain on-call 24/7 for the bad days.

The night that Steve is away, she phones us at 2:00 am. She is vomiting and frightened. I throw my winter coat on over my nightie, put boots on my bare feet and drive to Hobbit House. I curl around her tiny body as she sobs in bed: "I am trying to be brave, Mommy."

My love drops even deeper while grief grips my breath. I hold her boney body in my strong arms as she cries herself to sleep. At sunrise I sneak out, hoping that her morning ritual and anticipation of

Toronto friends coming for the day will help her. Later that day, when her friends have gone and she waits for Steve to bring her dinner, she calls. Her voice is bright. Sweet Laura relates how she has done most of her Christmas shopping online. She says we will all love her gifts. Her joyous giving heart finds gifts that are unique and thoughtful. I hang up and cry uncontrollably on the basement floor.

Melissa arrives for the holiday week and the two of them decorate the Christmas tree. I hear them laughing at the strange collection of ornaments they gathered over the years. "I hope I have a few more Christmases," says Laura, as she puts the white dove on the treetop. I turn away to hide the tears as my throat closes. "I hope you do too, my darling." I wonder how I will ever manage to get Christmas together this week.

In silence John and I take Laura for her last trip to the cancer clinic before Christmas. Since the appointments start at 7:45 she has slept at our place, only to awaken to a nagging headache and sore bones. The heart specialist reports that her heart is good but shows signs of chemo related stress. We visit her oncologist who compassionately reports that the scans show cancer in her spine, ribs, and thymus.

She has two years maximum of life. "Well, that is better than the few months Dr. Half-a-man predicted", she answers. Laura thanks her for doing all she has done to help her, picks up her 'never work again' papers and despondently, we drop her off at home to wait for Steve.

As we drive home, we speak of the alarming speed the cancer has spread. There is nothing we can do but witness her dying process. "FUCK cancer, fuck, fuck," I yell out to the early evening darkness as we drive home. John is mute.

Life without Laura? Why can't it be me? She is too young. Loving her increases my suffering. Can I love her enough to stay present to her needs as I witness her slow death? Where is my ground in death? Does death even have ground or is it empty space?

Christmas Eve, we decide to drive around the city park to see the lights. Melissa and Laura tell us they want to sleep in their childhood beds and wait to see if Santa still arrives. To their delight, he does and is as generous as always. For 35 years we have been blessed by wonderful Christmas mornings and this is no different. The gifts are thoughtful and given with love. Steve and Erich join us to celebrate dinner as a family. Laura, looking starkly beautiful with translucent white skin and wearing her pink 'fuck cancer' hat to keep her head warm, makes her usual wonderful gravy. She asks me to taste it as she can't taste anything since the brain radiation. Melissa quietly cleans up the kitchen after the meal, giving me time to enjoy my wine and post-dinner conversation. For a brief time, I disconnect from fear and grief. Love is the granite rock I stand on; it is the nectar breathing me, giving me the will to be here at this table with such love for Laura as she simultaneously dies and lives.

They all return to Laura's for the night. I dream:

I am in an environment of deep supporting ether.
It morphs into royal blue water. I breathe deeply as
I swim down into the depths, looking for Laura. I
intuit she is somewhere in this beautiful space.

Melissa and Erich return to Toronto. John and I prepare our New Year's dinner to take to the Woodman's, a ritual end-of-year meal we have shared for over 25 years. Laura and Steve quietly celebrate at Hobbit House.

It is now January 2013; I hang on a cross of life. Motherlove in me will never leave when Laura dies. The impersonal star points me in a direction where all I have cherished in my personal subjective life dissolves in its light. Is this ego-death, detachment from my past? Whatever, it all feels like a living hell to me.

9

THE OPEN MOMENT

"And so the darkness shall be the light,
and the stillness the dancing."

January 2013

Laura feels yucky and her temperature rises. I cancel my trip to work in Mexico the following week. At 10:00 pm we take her to emergency, where the waiting room is full to overcapacity. At midnight we decide to leave and return for her scheduled 7:30 am appointment at the clinic. We share a joint, fall asleep, and wake up with clear heads. Dr. H. takes one look at Laura and immediately finds a hospital bed for her, orders an IV with antibiotics, and arranges for full body scans. She is furious with the hospital's refusal to admit her last night and assures us it will not happen again.

We visit Laura in the hospital the next morning. Her temperature had dropped to normal and after a mild steroid, her appetite returns.

When her Toronto friends arrive, she cheerfully greets them as we leave. Two days later she is released from hospital and comes to our home for lunch where her cousin and his new baby wait to see her. Holding the infant in her arms, Laura gazes into his eyes. She talks quietly to him as he gurgles in return: new life regarding dying life. The room goes silent. Reality sinks deeper into the hole in my chest. Her dreams of marriage, children and a wonderful career no longer exist. Can a person function without hope? I need a joint at night to endure what I cannot face, to comfort me, to soothe my aching soul, to love and care for her alongside John—until she dies.

We spend a whole day at the nuclear medicine clinic. Laura walks with dignity from one grueling test to another. Without complaint she drinks a horrible pink liquid needed to make her bones and organs light up from the inside so the machine can find new tumors. When we drop her off at Hobbit House her dearest friend from work greets her. Laura learns her cherished job is now advertised Canada-wide. Another beloved part of her life disappears.

Later in the week my dearest friend calls to tell me her breast cancer has metastasized to her brain. I fall deeper into darkness. At the Inquiry group I explore the darkness. I observe how my brain labels darkness as depression: this activates my solar plexus; I feel depressed. But what does darkness really feel like? I explore more subtle sensory experiences. To my surprise I say: "Darkness feels like deep peace, stillness, silence. It feels like death."

Instantly my attention separates from peaceful darkness. I recognize infantile webs of conditioning telling me that I must hold myself together or I will fall apart. Deeper insight touches a holding pattern of preverbal fear that believes if I totally relax, I will cease to exist. I need to fix the situation, but newly born, there is no 'I' that knows how. Crying, the instinctual response of a baby in pain, creates a feeling of being substantial and real. Intense crying transforms intolerable pain into an experience of a separate self. A sense of isolated helplessness knots into the seed of feared abandonment. Webs of anxiety become preverbal habits, frozen in time, stabilizing the experience of a separate physical body. Patterns of contractions remain safely buried in unconscious tension and infantile thinking. My adult waking awareness remains ignorant of the natural inborn, still born, subtle sensitivity and delicate receptivity.

However, when I relax and drop into interior silence, attention widens and deepens to apprehend a field of unconditioned Love. This Love never solidified into a separate physical form. It remains whole. Still born, I realize the dark seed at the center still exists and remains full of the familiar content of me. Aware of both, attention allows me the freedom to be still born in deep peace or an isolated suffering mother—a hole within the whole.

The predictable nature of familiar yet unconscious habits hold me together. I am thankful for the ego's function to filter out painful experiences of helplessness and vulnerability in the face of Laura's dying. If I don't inquire into the source of my ideas about death, I behave as if the childhood situation of helplessness is the same as the present moment. I project the past into the present. Have I lived according to an unconscious internalized manual for safe living? Now, beneath conventional thought, I am 'peace beyond understanding'.

A new sensitivity emerges; I feel human suffering as if it is my own. I don't like it, but I inquire into its uncomfortable nature. With attention planted in sensate awareness, a window of new clarity opens—a self-aware field of sensory intelligence ready to be realized, made real. I dream:

> *I am planting a black sunflower seed in radiant dark soil. I can't make the seed produce roots and grow, but I can be sensitive to its natural needs—plant it in a sunny spot and water it. The hard seed spit open. I watch it grow by itself, extend roots down into the black soil and reach up into the light. Vibrant green leaves branch outwards like solar panels to follow the sun. My tears are the only source of water.*

A few days later I wait with John and Laura for the nuclear medicine results. Following a pattern of deep breathing, I begin to feel spaciousness around me that intersperses with the field around Laura. I don't see phenomena, yet the space seems to have its own way of communion. I am emotionally numb but mentally calm and present. I listen: radiation shrunk the brain tumors; the chemo dissolved tumors in her organs, and the fluid around her heart and lungs is gone. However, her thinning bones remain untouched by the various palliative treatments. Bone strengthening treatments are ordered. After dropping Laura off at her Hobbit House, John takes my hand and whispers: "We will have her a little while longer."

I dream that night:

Our family silently sits in a huge open restaurant waiting for our meal. A large creature, a cross between a crocodile and a manatee, arrives at the door. I realize the creature is my personal pet and let her in. She curls herself around my chair and gazes up into my eyes. I love its big, happy, smiling, contented face, and, although mute, I am intimately in tune with it.

I wake up savoring my unconditioned love for this good natured, simple, nonverbal beast. I intuit she supports me with her specific form of somatic and voiceless intelligence.

A new dynamic love spreads through me. In BodySoul workshops I hear women speak of hating parts of their bodies, particularly the upper thighs where strength is felt and, in the belly, where creativity is born. I remember cursing my imperfect 'ugly' dancer's body. Before Christopher's stillbirth, I unconsciously believed a son would redeem me of my mother's deeply entrenched belief of her inferiority to men. Mom's dark sadness held her fundamental belief that her function was to serve men. Without an awareness of the great love hidden inside living flesh, my mom embodied the unquestioned collective mindset of women's inferior nature reinforced by religious dogma. The loving, mute creation, the manatee of my dreams, substantiates the dynamic, intelligent, compassionate field creating physical existence.

Still born, instinctual sensory intelligence, informs me that LIFE loves itSelf into being an infinite variety of living forms, flesh being only one specific form. This feeling radically differs from the compulsive thought that I must fix my imperfect body. Love for all incarnate Life replaces self-hate. Am I reclaiming the original landscape of my true nature, sleeping in the soul-soil of indigenous female flesh? Is this my function, to awaken to living, intelligent, female soul-flesh? Is this love related to earth-centered awareness?

March 2013

I continue to drive Laura to alternative treatments for her comfort. On the road she shares how she no longer feels resistance to the invisible space around her. She says the man who was hired to replace her at work is weak, yet she feels gratitude for his continuing the projects she implemented. The music in her voice gives me hope. Her joy expands, filling the car with presence. Maybe there is hope.

Perhaps she is teaching me how to die in order to live. She is like a peapod splitting down her body to release new seeds of Life. I feel young in the presence of her old soul's vitality and all-embracing love.

I drop over to Hobbit House after exercise class. Three friends sit on her bed, sharing stories of jobs, babies, relationships, while Laura faces more drugs, side effects, and death. The presence of the manatee's love embraces my sorrow, while the crocodile aspect sleeps in the corner.

Laura tolerates the low doses of oral chemo and steroids. Her appetite returns, though she tastes nothing after the radiation. John and I decide to take the train to Toronto for a cancer-free weekend with friends and cousins. We attend art galleries, go out for meals, and take the train home, first class for the meal. The dinner, served with wine and liqueurs, helps us soften our entry into reality.

April 2013

We take Laura to her appointment with the oncologist. New scans reveal multiple lesions in Laura's liver. She asks to be dropped off in the park by the river. She walks away from the car, utterly alone and crying. We are devastated. After dinner she calls from Hobbit House. She doesn't want to be alone anymore. She knows she is dying. We drive over and wait for Steve to arrive in the evening.

"I need to go to the island the minute the ice is out!"

She will spend the summer with us. Joy and grief dance through me. Her presence etches into my heart, weaving her eternal imprint inside me, along with all her grief.

10

BEDROCK REALITY

"Life and death are but different phases of being.
You are part of the Eternal Life."

–Paramahansa Yogananda

May 2013

Early May we step onto the soul-soil of Colenso's sacred land. As Laura runs down to the front rocks and beach, John and I burst into tears. Last year we left with little hope of Laura being with us. Now, in her bare feet, she walks down to the children's beach and into the icy water. Joyously she splashes water as if baptizing herself in the holiness of wilderness. In the heat of the day she goes for a short swim, testing her lung capacity. Later, Steve, Melissa and Erich join us. That evening we watch wet snow pile up on the sundeck, reminding us it is not yet summer. We play board games, work on a puzzle, and read. When the warmth returns, Erich and Melissa disappear for a long island stroll where Erich proposes. Over a joyous meal we celebrate with them, along with honoring John's 70th birthday. How I treasure each moment, knowing it will be John's last birthday with Laura. As John and I clean up the kitchen, Steve leaves for London and Melissa and Erich take Laura for a sunset paddle in the canoe. The next morning Laura slowly walks alone on the island paths, crying. She knows she will never marry nor have children. We share her deep loss of the future she expected.

Now alone with us she spends her days outside in the warm spring sun. With her creativity destroyed from brain radiation and her mind dulled by painkillers, she can no longer read novels nor write her books. Instead, she reads gossip magazines about Hollywood stars. At the end of May she starts to vomit regularly. Her stomach isn't right, and the headaches return. Are the brain tumors growing? After a long phone conversation with her doctor, we decide to return to the city. The palliative team can reassess what new drugs will help manage the latest onset of uncomfortable symptoms.

The day before returning to the city, I take an early morning island walk. I notice dew drops coalescing on the thin spider webs between branches. The angle of the rising sun transforms the droplets into mini crystals of glistening rainbow colors. Each color reflects a tone; an inner atmosphere that I sense lives in me. Breathing in the color, I absorb its essence. I feel part of all I see, a form of joyful oneness. Yet, I am also a separate type of awareness inside the oneness. Whatever I am and whatever nature is weaves into a dynamic sense of self-awareness. My flesh absorbs, radiates, exists and knows. I am peaceful.

Judgement quickly takes over my joy with words that say I am just avoiding what is happening in our life. Words tell me grief has made me crazy.

Once back in London I dream:

I climb a rugged mountain and sit on the stone peak. I woman arrives and tries to knock me off. "You don't belong here." I hold firm. "I climbed this mountain and I deserve to sit here." The woman's face transforms into my younger self. She wants us to stay safe, small and ignorant of the eagle-eye view from the mountain with spacious clarity and ether to breathe.

I practice skills I participated in during ontological sessions in 1980. I learned to shift awareness from subjective thoughts to the impersonal field space above my head. Through repetition over the years, I can sustain attention in the field. I engage a more objective perception of life. Rather than worrying, I notice my hands washing dishes. I like the feel of warm soapy water. Sometimes I don't think at all, yet I know I am fully awake. I step outside compulsive thinking and looping self-talk.

Sometimes I glimpse invisible subtle insights weaving my thoughts, emotions and sensations into a sense of deep knowing. Isolated patterns of sluggish energy collapse into a coherency, a new dance where subjective/objective perceptions harmonize into a flow of unfamiliarity. New pathways of insight, understanding of old patterns and creative ideas enliven me. My capacity to observe intimate sensory experiences from a more objective view, engages more functions simultaneously. The tension felt in highly emotional reactivity, once seen from a more objective view, tend to melt like butter in the sun. Relaxing into this sensation, I take the next step. I feel utterly human in my vulnerable self.

I dream:

I clean an old dock that has been in the bottom of a deep lake for many years. I prepare it as a landing site for boats and perhaps a helicopter. Scrubbing the years of green slime off the wood, I sense I am prey to an invisible beast. I know it is Laura's cancer. A rainbow appears and I think that if I enter that rainbow, the beast will rise up and eat me. A voice speaks: "Birth is the first great sacrifice of the eternal Being. The second is the terrible gift of knowledge that you will die, and so will all that you have loved since your birth."

I wake up remembering the great forgetting mystics speak about. It happens at birth. Does death bring a great remembering? Perhaps my saltwater tears of motherlove carry ancient wisdom. I feel the boundless gift of being Laura's mom for 33 years, balanced with the binding reality of grief in my core. I remember feeling the unconditional love during my three pregnancies for whoever grew in my womb. My heart expanded. Motherlove knew how to care deeply for someone beyond myself and also knew to care and tend to all Life outside my physical self.

My children belong to Life. I too belong to Life. Releasing the sense of possessiveness—my children, my body, my home, my island, my Life—I begin to withdraw projections. I realize my need for Laura to live is not what Life needs.

John arranges with the burial service, a Simple Alternative, to pick up Laura's body when she dies. Years ago, before cancer, we shared with our daughters our wishes around death. When Tim died, we had another family conversation. Laura said she wanted the tiny wooden urn on her mantle with his ashes to be cremated with her. After a frightening night of her coughing and vomiting, I arrange for Laura to sign the forms for her home death at Hobbit House. I download the forms and see that many questions have been covered in former family talks.

It is a terrible day. Laura welcomes the heath care nurse with her usual presence. Her bone body is propped up in her bed with soft white pillows. She wears her pink 'fuck cancer' hat and pretty earrings. Youthful beauty shines through her translucent skin.

When the woman says the process will take two afternoons, Laura's anger rises like a lioness after her prey. I know her vulnerable tears are inside her rage. With my tight jaw, and squinting eyes, I speak: "We will do this in one hour. Most of the questions have been dealt with. Here are the completed forms with the funeral home, cremation information, and the sign off with the doctor's name for when she dies."

I am a great mother bear protecting her baby. All Laura has to do is check off the pages and sign them.

Death, the iced-in secret, creeps into the room, an enormous beast coming to annihilate us. My flesh weeps with her. "Do you agree, Laura?" asks the nurse. With tears of rage and grief, Laura nods her head, signs the papers in her 'important unreadable signature' and hands them over. I immediately escort the woman out of the room. The hellish process takes an hour. As I relax, I know it is a difficult afternoon for the nurse. I feel compassion for her, for Laura, for me and the situation. Laura's wish to die in her own home is set in place. I feel hope drop away like autumn leaves. Something crawls into bed with Laura, holds her, and weeps. I wait for Steve to arrive.

Laura calls the next morning. After sleeping for 15 hours, she woke up with a rash and calls her Palliative team. Within an hour we welcome them at Hobbit House. This compassionate team will now care for her, along with other night nurses, when needed. The rash, a sign of liver failure, requires new drugs. Laura explains she needs to go back to the island. They agree: "You will go on 'Hospice Vacation'. We are available by phone and email

24/7. A local team at the Parry Sound hospital will be alerted to your needs and made available to help us and you. We will loan you an oxygen machine to take to the island."

I see Laura relax, especially when they tell her they have patients who live several years on Hospice Vacation. Island here we come!

We call Melissa. She wants to be with Laura and drives immediately to London to take her to an afternoon cranial sacral treatment. Home alone for the afternoon, John and I start planning for Laura's Tribute; we can't call it a Celebration of Life. The CEO of the Y, Laura's boss man, phones. We share ideas about the venue for her Tribute, figuring 200 friends would be there. The Y expects over a 1000! She is loved by many former campers, staff, the management team and board members. Everyone loves her, including camper parents. The Y agrees to arrange the venue, the program design, organize all the technical equipment, create a slideshow and order the food. Overwhelmed with gratitude, we agree. No wonder Laura loved the Y. They share the responsibility for caring for one another, something Laura lives naturally.

John and I collect our old family albums from the basement. We select pictures of Laura's life from birth to now. It is exhausting to review her life, knowing it is for her funeral. She doesn't want it to be held in a church where a minister changes the name of the dead and repeats everything else. She asks that her ceremony be uniquely about her and what she loves.

June 2013

Melissa and I chat as I drive our car back to the island. Laura sleeps in the back seat. John follows in Lady Red, Laura's car, with Darth Vapor, the oxygen machine, and the medical supplies. On arrival, Laura, who loves to cook, makes us a pizza and salad to celebrate her return. At sunset we decide to walk the island together, but just after starting, Laura vomits. We turn back. She takes morphine for her headache. It doesn't work. She tries a powerful nose spray. It knocks her out. On waking, she laughs, pain free: "Wow I could make a fortune selling this stuff on the streets!"

Melissa sleeps with her sister in the king-sized bed, agreeing to handle the night pill duty. Laura sleeps in late. Melissa rises early to mark papers.

We quietly work outside. On waking, Laura is lethargic and mourns her reality—being without pain means being without energy and mental clarity. She monitors her drugs, trying to find the balance between pain level and mental clarity. When 'Nurse Melissa' returns to the city to work, Steve arrives with his office work to take over the night duty. Laura is delighted. She adores his company.

Darth Vapor hums in the front room, providing a steady source of oxygen to ease Laura's breathing, its 30-foot tube snaking after her. She can wander throughout the cottage and the front deck. With her portable oxygen tank, she can even go on family outings.

Laura needs people her own age. When Melissa or Steve can't be with her, other dear friends arrive. Though her mind is slower, she seems better physically. She loves the company of her friends as much as they love being with her. Each one agrees to be her personal nurse, sleep in the king-size bed, and be the night duty nurse. We remain on call at the end of the hall. A quiet sadness sinks in as we watch Laura being cared for by her loving friends. We hit bedrock reality.

On a calm July morning, when the sacredness of LIFE silences the mind and stills the soul, Laura asks me to take her out into the open water. In the small boat, I drive her to a smooth pink rock-shoal, once the root of an ancient mountain. Surrounded by eternal space, she sits quietly on the rock at the water's edge. With her toes in the water, she stares at an empty horizon. I walk barefoot on the warm rocks, exploring small pools where tadpoles grow. As the morphine wears off, and her breathing becomes difficult, she turns her gaze from the open water with its vast horizon: "It's time to go now, Mom".

As she ties the boat to the dock, she announces, "Let's call it Magic Pond Island". I agree it is a good name, knowing she will never return. Later in the week, she stands on the rocks looking down at her favorite swimming spot she calls Noggin's Lagoon. "If I come back in an urn, Mom, I want my ashes scattered here." I nod in silence, my throat closing up. The windchime hanging from the pine tree above sings in the gentle breeze.

Melissa celebrates her July birthday in Toronto where she and Erich are in the process of moving into their new home. She is relieved that the increase in morphine controls Laura's bone pain, giving her time to enjoy her visiting friends. She loves that Laura can even enjoy short swims, depending on her breathing capacity. Near the end of July, Steve drives Laura home for a week in London. She desperately wants to go to a friend's wedding. When they arrive back at the island, Steve proudly shows us a picture to see how beautiful she looked. She is radiant. He says she was the life of the party. However, when alone, he shares that the bride gave Laura her private room. There she vomited, rested, connected to her oxygen machine, regained some strength and returned to the party. In private he shares Laura has panic attacks when she vomits and can't catch her breath. She can't breathe the polluted London air.

Later at the cottage, sitting with Laura on the dock, she shares: "My life is now a downward spiral ending in death, Mom. My friends are living exciting lives with good jobs, great partners and one is pregnant."

I am silenced. I love her so much. I can't take her pain away or fix her life. I am bone tired with emotional exhaustion and an aching heart. I try to respond to her needs by staying present to her energy and pain levels in the face of cancer's relentless intensity. I salvage vestiges of her joy in moments, but it feels like so little.

Dying has its own timing; we can't predict when her day will arrive. My life feels bittersweet, especially when Melissa lives with us. Laura now needs 21 pills a day to control her symptoms. They make her dopey but the pain level endurable. Moments throughout the day, her wonderful soul emerges in joy. Swimming still brings her great pleasure though she can only do a few strokes before returning to shore for oxygen.

Before cancer she and Melissa swam together around the whole island, a good 40-minute trip. Sometimes tears roll down her face when she holds things she loves. Saying farewell to her island cousins is excruciating for her. So much is put into perspective as we see life through her eyes. Love keeps us breathing.

August 13

On the morning of my 67th birthday, I wake Laura up for her pills. Her thin arms reach up around my neck and with her morphine smile she mumbles, "I love you Mommy, Happy Birthday." We linger, feeling the love flow through our arms and into our hearts. She falls asleep in my arms.

Melissa, after wishing me a happy birthday, shares the wedding plans she and Erich worked on the night before. I express my happiness for her. I feel the stretch between death and new beginnings. I walk alone to the back of the island to meditate. There I find John crying. We hold each other and sob. Our daughters have radically changed: Melissa, a teacher about to marry and hopeful for a family; Laura, drugged on morphine for bone pain, steroids for appetite and brain tumors, Ativan for anxiety when she can't breathe, and relaxants for muscle spasms caused by the cocktail of drugs.

Before returning to Toronto, Melissa and Erich create a wonderful birthday dinner. Laura manages to swallow a spoonful. Opening her gift to me, my hands feel the softness of a purple cashmere sweater. "I wore it for a full day, Mommy and filled it with my love so you can feel it forever."

Swallowing my grief, I hold her tiny body in my arms. When will I have the courage to wear it without my heart unravelling? Thankfully, my cousins arrive with a freshly baked wild-blueberry pie. I breathe in the blessing. When Melissa hugs her to leave the next morning, Laura sobs in her arms. Melissa tries to console her, saying she is returning in a few weeks. We realize, like Laura, the final goodbye hug is approaching. How does one endure that? Keep breathing...in two three...out two three...in two three...out two three...Standing beside Laura, we watch the kids' boat disappear around the point. Later, I hear John reading to Laura in her bed until she falls asleep.

September 2013

During the day when Laura sleeps, John works outside on the land. I meditate and write. Looking out at the horizon, powerful waves crash into the shoals, shooting sprays of water high into the air. In my journal I write:

"So, this is real grief. Sadness feels bottomless. Nothing helps as I wait for darling Laura to die. Now, she rests peacefully and full of addictive drugs. When will they stop working? I ponder Buddha's story about a mother who can't stop grieving the death of her child. He suggests she knock on doors and find a home without grief. Two years later, she returns to the Buddha: 'There are no homes free of grief.' I realize that expanding the heart to include both self-compassion and compassion for all things, is the only way through for me. This compassion is not personal: my flesh silently accepts and loves all that is, just as it is, including what our family lives now. I do nothing to make it happen. It reveals itself in the holes of my heart. The more vulnerable I feel the more it seeps out. This is the Love that is enough to let her die when the pain is no longer controllable. Will my center endure? Silence speaks: 'Keep focusing on the breath…it breathes you into life…*you* don't breathe… *Life* breathes Laura into life. One day it will exhale her out. It is not yours or hers to control. There is no how to. Living all will come to pass.'"

I remember 9/11 when I was teaching an international group in Devon, England. When the Twin Towers collapsed all communication was severed. No one knew what was happening. At the time Melissa was teaching in Mexico, Laura was at university, and John was alone at the island. I held myself together to help the group focus through the hours of unknowing. When the group broke for dinner, I ran up to the moors. Sitting alone on my morning meditation rock, surrounded by gorse, my body trembling, I cried out over the land: "How do we endure man's inhumanity to man?" A sheepdog appeared and licked away my salted tears. An old crone approached me, her hand-hued walking stick supporting her. "Keep crying my dear. Mother Earth can take it. My three sons died in the war; each day she absorbs my grief." Calling her dog, she leaves me to sit on the rock.

Today I am comforted by her wise words. Three sons lost to war: one daughter eaten by cancer. Life continues. But I want this nightmare of endless drugs and nightly vomiting to end. But, oh, I want her to live! My wanting wastes energy.

John feels the need to talk about Laura's upcoming 34th birthday. We decide to ask her.

"I want a big London party, a 'Staying Alive' celebration at the end of the month. According to statistics I am not supposed to be alive. I want more life, even if I am addicted to painkillers."

We agree to host it. It feels right. Her energy returns.

Steve arrives for her birthday week. This frees us to share meals with island friends, giving us a sense of normalcy. The weather on her birthday is clear, crisp with wild September winds. John suggests we take the boat through protected channels and walk a short trail to the high cliffs overlooking the open bay. Laura thinks she can do it and immediately prepares for the big outing. Sitting in the bow of the boat, a big smile on her face, I marvel at her radiance, her joy in feeling the rhythm of the waves, the wind in her face and the warmth of the sun. She is lost in reverie. Walking slowly, we make it to the high cliffs where the full impact of the west wind flings huge waves against the ancient rocks. The water explosions are exhilarating. Together we lift our arms up to the sky to sense the vital energy of Life filling our bodies. At bedtime, John reads her, *The Birthday Book*, by Dr. Seuss. She falls asleep smiling.

Her sadness in leaving the island is punctuated by her joy in planning her big event. On Facebook she puts out the invitation; the response is huge. Will our small house hold everyone? We leave the island on a cold day. The autumn wind has a crispy bite to it. Laura sits behind me, sheltered from the wind. She clutches Roary to her heart. Lifting his stuffed paw, he waves goodbye to her beloved island while her tears fall on his soft head. No mother should see her child suffer emotionally at this level. Her beloved Tim died nine years ago this September. Now it is her turn to release all she loves and holds dear in her being.

11

DARK NIGHT OF THE SOUL

*"There is no pain so great as the memory of joy
in present grief."*

–Aeschylus

September 2013

Once back in the city, Laura feels and looks better than when we left in May. She has gained weight and moves without much pain. Her headaches have lessened, and she doesn't vomit at night. Sharing this with Dr. S, he says this often happens in palliative care. Free of invasive treatments to kill cancer, the palliative drugs provide relief and quality of life. With Laura excited about her upcoming party, perhaps something new will enter our lives. John says he has more cracks in his heart. I dream I am ready to give birth.

I notice the space between objects more as a flowing dance than as invisible air. I intuit softer lenses in my eyes that make objects lose their solidness. On one level I feel like I am collapsing, returning to ground; simultaneously, on another level, I am able to sustain attention. Attention is more intense now than before the summer. Energetically I feel like water, two parts grief and one part present. The night before Laura's big event, a dream voice tells me:

> *"What you choose doesn't matter; the real LIFE dwells behind everything; the rest, a veil to cover truth."*

We prepare for Laura's 'Stayin Alive Party'. We expect over 100 friends, flying in from across the country to say hello and goodbye. The catered food is placed in the kitchen and dining room. In-laws and neighbors set up a bar on the front porch; the backyard table and chairs are cleaned; Roary books are for sale in the den. We are blessed with perfect weather. We wait for Laura to arrive.

The phone rings. Breathlessly one of Laura's friends calls; Laura has fallen and in terrible pain. John grabs his car keys while I call Steve to go immediately to Hobbit House. They transfer her to the car, drive to our house and carry her up the stairs where she lies on pillows on our bed. She is determined to greet her friends. Tim's sister guards the bedroom door, allowing small groups in for short periods. Laura greets them with a loving presence. Melissa mingles downstairs through the crowds now arriving to celebrate. John and I make sure the food and drinks are in full supply while constantly monitoring darling Laura. After two hours, she can no longer endure the pain. John calls an ambulance. Immediate family and beloved neighbors continue to host her party. John and I follow the ambulance.

For 15 hours, under bright florescent lights, we wait in a small consulting room for a surgeon. Since the hospital can't provide pain relief until she is seen by the doctor, we feed her morphine pills from her large bag of pills she carries with her. When the surgeon arrives, he apologizes for the long wait; a serious road accident kept all medical staff on overdrive. Laura asks if the surgery saved lives. On hearing the affirmative, she says: "It was worth my wait then."

After hearing about her cancer, her age, the party, how she fell, he realizes the degree of pain she has endured. He asks the 'difficult question' concerning her life expectancy. Surgery is not possible if the patient is dying. "I was to be dead two years ago. That's why I was celebrating my 34th birthday". He is stunned. "We will operate tonight". Closing her eyes in pain and gratitude, she whispers, "thank you". Orders are given; she is wheeled away behind metal doors. With nothing left for us to do, we go home. There is no evidence of the party. Family and neighbors put everything back in their place. Melissa, Erich, and Steve wait out the night at Hobbit House.

After enduring dreadful bone pain from cancer, before and after the surgery, the hospital palliative team finally arrives, 24 hours after her hip replacement. She requires a private room because her immune system is compromised. I sleep on the grey tile floor beside her bed, pushing the pain pump every two hours giving her uninterrupted sleep. At her home, John arranges the main floor to be set up with the hospital aides she needs in the bathroom. He locates a cane and a walker. He transforms her tiny den into a bedroom with her TV screen on her desk. A bed is placed in her dining room for sleep overs. A week later she arrives home from the hospital.

Looking around her beloved Hobbit House, tears well up in her eyes. "Well, I guess I get to experience old age, now." Four days later she walks with Melissa to the street corner and back, determined to heal and return to her independent life. She says fear is the architect of her limits. Always a risk-taker, she practices climbing the stairs to her bedroom where she and Steve can be together again at night. Melissa and Erich return to Toronto to teach. With Steve, we can manage her 24/7 home care with daily visits from hospice nurses and her special Y friends.

I am slowly losing what I love the most, a beloved child. I tenderly face what I can hardly endure, motherlove grief. "Mom, it should be me caring for you in this bed, not you caring for me." Reversals of archetypes create chaos in my psyche. I am compelled to walk in both directions—into life and into death—to uncover a functional mid-point. I thought this was something to accomplish, a destination to achieve. Now, I maintain attention on just breathing, on being present moment by moment and on what is needed to survive. When sitting with Laura, I am calm; back home, I collapse in tears of exhaustion.

However, sometimes in meditation, I find myself slipping underneath my grief into an intimate experience of grace, a vast, all-encompassing Love.

Here I function without collapsing into tears. I sense a new level of deep trust—loving kindness in the universe? Trusting this great Love, I feel it balances the deepening awareness of death. I am both. I am neither. I just am. I exist, speechless, alert and functional.

October 2013

Thanksgiving weekend Melissa and Erich stay in the basement apartment of Hobbit House. As Laura dies upstairs in her home, they make their final plans for a Christmas wedding. They book a small venue, an historic home in London, for December 28th. It will be decorated beautifully for Christmas. With lists in hand, they set to work. As they order food, I arrange for a block of hotel rooms for the guests; John calls the local school bus company to transport guests between the hotel and the venue. Erich agrees to make a sound tape and arrange for the DJ. Melissa agrees to handle all other details. When John and Steve care for Laura, I prepare invitations for our family, Erich for his family and Melissa for their friends. In two hours we finish. By the end of the Thanksgiving holiday, the wedding arrangements are completed. Melissa's bridesmaids in Toronto agree to take her dress shopping, something I have dreamed of since she was little and know I can't. As Melissa hugs me goodbye she says: "If I do all this with love in my heart, Mom, I'm OK. It is the time to do it." Waving goodbye, I am deeply thankful for her in my life. Somehow, she balances Laura's dying, her heavy teaching load and her wedding plans with grace. I hold her in my heart. She is losing her beloved sister, her dearest friend, her maid of honor, if…only…focus on the breath… uncover the mid-point, the both/and…the balancing point… both and neither…inhale.

John insists I go to the Chicago BodySoul conference to speak to the leadership group as planned a year ago. Before leaving, a dream voice tells me:

"Keep scrubbing the sacred temple floors."

At the conference I speak of the paradigm of unity consciousness and Jung's concept of the bi-polar nature of the psyche. I discuss the necessity of bringing focused attention to meditative practices involving sensory awareness free of labels. I mention the need for maturing emotional intelligence and soul readiness. I feel calm and clear.

Back in London, I spend the next two nights at Hobbit House, relieving John and Steve. I face my dying child. Now 95 pounds, Laura practices walking without a cane and forces herself to nibble food throughout the day. She watches videos late into the night and sleeps until noon. In the sunroom, her old dining room, I sketch, meditate, work with dream images and write in my journal. I want her to live—what I hope for is hopeless…"and do not hope, for hope would be hope for the wrong thing". (T. S. Eliot) There is no 'how to live' without hope; rather, something other takes over and breathes me.

John and I are slowly dying with Laura. I marvel at Steve's playful loving way with her and John's bottomless compassion. Every night I find love notes from him on my pillow. Our love grows deeper and more encompassing. Even death can't separate us now. Our 43 years together creates the bedrock of love strong enough to uncover a pathway through to Laura's death…and perhaps, even beyond.

November 2013

Before I leave for my exercise class, Laura looks into my eyes: "Mom, I think my body is losing function, breaking down." As I leave, John shares with me that last night Laura slept for two hours, vomited seven times and was in pain. The drugs have shut her bowels down. Nothing works…she can't breathe properly, has waves of bone pain, feels nauseous, dopey, and constantly thirsty. I go numb. No self-pity. Life is what it is.

The endurance to stay with her suffering and not cut my love off in fear matures. My heart silently weeps, yet it appears to survive absorbing the reality of her suffering. I sense an impersonal lens seeing the situation without judgement, without emotional drama. My silent tears are tiny crystals reflecting rainbow colors. The situation demands I be flexible, present and caring without collapsing. Laura has too much to carry without my suffering. I just want to gather her in my arms and nourish her with the wine of my old age. But I can't. It is now too painful for her to move.

I remember learning about woman's blood mysteries in Neumann's book, *The Great Mother: An Analysis of the Archetype*. When menstrual blood stops, a fetus forms in the womb. Once born, blood transforms into breast milk, the perfect food to nourish new life. At the time I dreamt:

> *I was an elderly woman with breasts full of wine.*
> *Anyone with an empty cup could fill theirs up.*

When breastfeeding, I knew my body seamlessly and naturally transmitted both spirit and physical nourishment to the baby in my arms. Communion, union of mother-infant-spirit-matter, lived in me, in the baby, in the milk and in the field. I did nothing but show up and savor the experience. Is my aging wine-spirit nourishing Laura? Sitting here, doing nothing, are we in communion—ONE inside the now?

A honey-colored impulse, rising up my body, infuses me with compassion. Naked acceptance of Laura's dying opens me into a field of all-encompassing Love.

Nothing is prettied up to deny death's truth. The starkness, like a fierce north wind, slices through my conditioned habit of avoiding what is real. When I think a situation is too painful to face, I tend to cut it out of my sight. What lies beneath the niceties of surface talk? In silence I commune with Laura: It is OK to die, my darling, to end your suffering, even if it means leaving all that you love. Trust the soul's decision to release you into the Absolute. I will too, my love.

Before I leave for my night off, I check on John. I see the suffering on his face as he sits in the semi-darkness, holding Laura's hand. She drifts off gasping for breath. Suffering weaves into the fabric of our flesh, sustaining molecules, holding organs in place. Oh, how I will miss her walking into our home, her radiant smile, the sound of her voice, her laughter, her sense of humor, her wonderful full-body hugs. How I will miss seeing John's joy when he greets her with his warm, inviting embrace.

Perhaps my grieving these losses now is part of motherlove transitioning to elder love, from personal grief to impersonal world sorrow, not as an idea, but as a living interior dynamic shared by humanity. In her dying, perhaps Laura leads the way into our future we cannot yet imagine.

On my night with her, she struggles to speak through her swollen cracked lips: "I didn't think cancer was all that serious at first. Perhaps that thinking brought me time to enjoy what life I had left. I can't try to go back to the island this summer. I don't need to anymore. I'll always be there, won't I, Mom? I'll never have to leave."

"Yes, my darling. I will meet you there, as I promised."

"I can't find the exit sign to take me out, Mommy. How do I stop this? I need it to end."

She closes her eyes and drifts off into a silent, still world.

A voice whispers: "Breathing has become a straw that your drowning self clings to." I drop into an attitude of impersonal love. My interior space grows into a black crystal floating in a pulsing sphere of liquid gold. I sense a communion between my intimacy with Laura and the impersonal face of death—a brief moment suspended in the eternal timelessness of Divine Love.

The palliative team arrives early the next morning. An IV is inserted into her belly, the only place left with enough flesh to support a needle. All pain drugs, including steroids, are administered through saline and a pain pump. Too weak to walk to the bathroom, they order a bedside commode. All attempts of privacy are gone. I hear her say to Dr. S: "Last night the pain was so awful I prayed to god to let me die and I don't even believe in God." A new regime of end-of-life-pills, coma inducing drugs, is added to the saline. That night she is so ill. She feels the pain yet remains fully alert and can't wake up or move—a curse worse than death! We throw out the new solution. By afternoon she is more alert and relieved. When the palliative team arrives I hear her say: "I just need a few good hours a day to make life worthwhile. If there is only pain, I can't see the point of living anymore."

There is no need for Laura to buy her dress for Melissa's wedding. I accept what is. When John and I are at home together, we continue to plan and collect photos for Laura's Tribute. We then shift focus from the grief to re-focus on wedding details. Darling Melissa shares that she has said goodbye to Laura so many times this past year that whatever the timing of her death, she wants her wedding to happen. She wants children. Time tics away. A small flame flickers in my heart. I hear her deep need to get on with her life with Erich. I love her so much.

Planning the wedding provides pillars to let the river of sorrow flow through. When I am with Laura, I breathe to stay present as she struggles for breath. She no longer is able to type on her Blackberry; her swollen fingers won't work. She closes her eyes to mourn the end of her last link with her friends. Her sight is going; her feet swell into footballs with the saline drip. Her tissues break down and lose function. The morphine affects her ability to form words. She wants to eat and can't. She can't sit up to vomit. She can't die: she can't live….breathe.

One morning she shares with me that the night nurse talked nonstop at her. I decode her words: "I'd never judge another for their need to talk about themselves. She was very motherly in her help. I appreciated it and told her. She said she was a mother to all. She left happy, despite her complaints that my house has no TV, no microwave, and what was she supposed to do for her eight-hour night shift."

I sit beside beloved Laura, holding her white hand in mine, watching the slow rise and fall of her breath. I shift focus and look outside her window where John put a bird feeder. Laura smiles when the little feathered creatures fly in to feed. Beyond the feeder, I focus on the huge oak tree in her back yard. I call her Mother Earth and thank her for her strength, her presence, her solid and stable nature. Laura awakens.

"Don't let go of my hand, Mommy. I don't know where I am. I am not in pain."

"I have your hand, darling. I won't leave you. One of us is always here at night, in your upstairs bedroom. The night nurse will get us anytime you want."

"What happens if I don't make it to the end of the week? I used to feel like a person. Now I don't."

How cruel it is to keep her alive! Thank heavens our dogs never had to endure this. She is dying and we can't speed it up and put her out of her suffering. "Comfort is no longer an option, Mom. If I lie perfectly still, the pain isn't as bad."

Her palliative team apologizes to us. They say the young ones take a long time to die because whatever is cancer free remains strong and functional.

Three weeks from now is Melissa's wedding. Laura's bedsore grows deeper, closer to bone. A new 'breathing bed' arrives as the pressure on her bones protruding from her spine break through her tissue-paper skin. One night her whole body contracts into spasms. She screams. John grabs her tightly in his arms as I wrap mine around them both with all my strength. It is surreal. If only assisted dying were legal! No one should have to endure this decay!

Oddly, John reports he has never curled so well. In yoga class my balance is remarkable. Perhaps life, demanding that we stay in the moment, holds us steady, alert, poised, ready and anticipating whatever is next. We have no surplus energy to even worry. What is needed, we do. I am not sure if this is automatic pilot or total presence. Is the rhythm of breathing the catalyst keeping me alive?

Laura's morphine levels increase. Ativan is her friend. Some days she manages to sit up at her dining room table and eat two or three grapes or a mouthful of yogurt. Assisting her as she takes the five steps back into her bed takes so long, each step requiring her full focus and energy. Her dearest friend, who stays with her when we exercise, tells me Laura isn't quite ready to die; there are things she still needs to do. Melissa phones me in tears about Laura not being at her wedding as her Maid of Honor. In meditation, I connect to the spaciousness that nourishes whatever is left of me. I am nothing but a momentary expression of the Absolute in a finite form. I will accompany Laura on a journey of compassionate return to source. Who or what we will be remains a mystery. The rainbow image from her birth reappears and I hear Laura's voice from years ago, long before cancer: "Mommy, we came here together."

The increased levels of morphine add to Laura's confusion. She grows anxious. She needs to know the plans around the wedding, who will care for her, where will we be. She frequently directs her anger and frustrations at me when I give her another needle, bring her bits of food, and encourage her to drink. How does one die with one daughter and celebrate marriage with another? No how-to. I am humbled by the veracity of death and life. I still exist on the side of the living.

Holding her hand as she drifts off into sleep, morphine dripping into her belly, I watch her brow relax as her breath becomes more even. Staring out at Grandmother Tree, I too drop into rhythmic breathing. The tree's great strength and naked branches reach into the clear winter sky. Calm breathing silences her pain. I unwind into stillness. I write in my journal:

"I realize how the events of each day shape me into a caring mother, where love for Laura guides me to act with infinite kindness and presence. To suffer consciously requires a capacity to love with a unique human heart, beating in space-time reality, while dwelling in the impersonal, spaciousness of death. The one who breathes at the crossroad between death and life becomes a tiny pinprick, a pulsating miniscule hole punctured into the darkness of a midnight sky. I am that hole, and I am the whole midnight sky—w/hole. Does Divine Love bloom in the open heart of a mother who holds a dying child?

Is this the experience of Mary, Mother of Christ, with her crucified son on her lap? Why does no one focus on the quality of her loss, her motherlove? Is the trinity of mother-daughter-holy spirit less than the father-son-holy spirit? Are they all part of the same phenomena? The bleeding heart, the intersection of life and death, the symbol of the cross, motherlove— one day I might know."

A dream:

I am wearing my life jacket as I swim towards the horizon of the ocean. My head is above the surface. My sunglasses have a small hole in each lens, a pinhole. The hole, like a porthole, focuses my attention as I observe situations emerge from the ocean, become events and sink back down below the surface. I accept all I see with compassion. Life is what it is. A voice speaks: "Be it a wedding or a funeral, you will die into the one who swims in this ocean of Life".

December 23 is a bitterly cold still night with warnings of snow. We go to the lawyer, transfer Hobbit House into John's name, and arrange for Laura's care during the two days of the wedding. John makes the phone calls to finalize her cremation. I cook Christmas day dinner to take to Hobbit House for our last family dinner. Laura rallies with

Steve and Melissa caring for her, rather than her aging parents. Our hearts relax. Laura will not die on Melissa's wedding day.

We decide to order in pizza on Christmas Eve. Laura is tearful as we share the minimal Christmas meal in her home. Opening our family presents, the love is palpable. As always, Laura managed to find meaningful gifts for each of us. She especially delights in John's gift to her that she saw a year ago at the auction house. I treasure her great joy in giving and her excitement when she finds the perfect gift.

The night before the wedding, a night nurse and Steve stay with Laura, giving us the evening to be with Melissa. I stay up with Melissa as John goes to bed. She wants to smoke some marijuana so she can sleep. Through laughter she announces: "A mink stole covering my shoulders for outdoor winter photos would finish off my perfect dress". I go to the basement closet and to Melissa's amazement her grandmother's beautiful mink stole appears. She tries it on—perfect fit. Now all is complete. We sleep well.

The weather gods are with us on December 28th. A covering of new snow sparkles in warm bright sunlight. The guests are happy with the hotel and love the school bus rides back and forth from the event. The service is bathed in the afternoon light streaming through the windows. The food is delicious. Melissa and Erich are radiantly happy. The speeches are delightfully entertaining and the dancing lively and fun. The guest's share that it was the most real wedding they had ever been to. My heart sings knowing Melissa will have positive memories of this day. I am thankful pictures are taken. I have no memory of it, except when John broke down in his speech for the bride. When he mentioned Laura's name, tears broke forth from his tired eyes. I ran to his side, held his hand and, as he cried, I tried to recall what he wanted to say. Melissa was disappointed that I rescued him, but nothing in me could let him stand alone in such deep, naked sorrow and weep.

12

SITTING ON THE RIM OF LIFE

"There is a journey you must take. It is a journey without destination. There is no map. Your soul will lead you. And you can take nothing with you."

–Meister Eckhart

January 2014

Melissa and Erich leave to begin their new life in Toronto. Laura weeps as Melissa assures her she will call daily and will be returning in two weeks. With tears flowing down her face, she can no longer cry openly: the bedsore hurts too much when she moves. I intuit she is afraid. More drugged than ever, she still breathes. Comfort is no longer an option. Even when she is drugged to oblivion, she hears our voices, yet she can only make sounds and murmur half-shaped words. I hear her mumble: "I am living death, Mommy. This is worse than pain… I can't do it anymore. I am trying and I can't…. I need to go ice cold…. Help me, Mommy. I don't want strangers in my house. You must hear me, you must—only family and Steve."

She is in pain and doesn't understand what is happening. I spend the night holding her hand. She winces when I push the new pain medication button. Her bone body is full of chemicals. Forty pounds of her is already lost. I go to join John in the front room. Through tears he says: "If I had an end of life pill now, I would give it to her. I want to make her heart stop and don't know how."

"And, as an act of love, I would give her the water to swallow it. Where is that brain tumor that was to kill her in two months and now a year later look at her? Fuck to anyone who says euthanasia is wrong. Maybe if they were suffering like her, they too would beg for the death pill. I am helpless. I want her back and I want her dead. If this is what it means to be in God's hands, screw God! We're hanging on the cross of Life." Tenderly we cry in each other's arms.

She screams. Total body spasms contract her into a tight ball. "FUCK!" she screams sitting up in shock. We embrace her and gently ease her back onto the bed.

She starts to laugh: "I hope that isn't my last word!"

Early the next morning the hospice team arrives. They are infinitely patient with her as she tries to communicate. I hear her say to Dr. S: "Dying is scary."

"Do you want to talk about the process? "

"No thanks. I have been told several times over the past two years, and I am still here. No one is right. Conscious sedation is worse than death. Confusion is worse than pain. I am fully aware, but I can't talk any more except in groans and these tiny movements. I pray to die and I don't know who I am asking."

We learn she has reached a new plateau. It could be days, or months. The palliative nurse resets the drips, changes the dressing on her bedsores, and writes out a new schedule of drugs she can take orally. With the new regime, Laura's mind is clearer and her ability to shape words improves.

Spiritual friends from California write to say they will accompany Laura to the life/death membrane when her time comes. She smiles when I share this. She trusts their stories of dying more than the specialists. She smiles when I tell her a greeting community awaits her. "Ah, that's good news, Mom. I like these stories best. They seem more real." She closes her eyes. The 'breathing bed' hisses and sighs, rises and falls with wave-like ripples to distribute her weight away from the bedsores on her spine.

After numerous phone calls to homecare agencies, we finally find an open- hearted, bright young woman. Though already a grandmother, she is Laura's age. Laura relates to her immediately, letting her take over her personal care. With more phone calls, and pleading our case, the agency lets her stay with Laura for 12-hour shifts, seven days a week. She loves being Laura's personal companion and caregiver and appreciates the extra money. She just graduated as a Personal Support Worker (PSW) and was top in her class. Without asking, she quietly does the little things she is not hired to do— dusting, dishes, making lists of things we need to buy, folding laundry, reminding us when to give Laura her pills. We welcome her into our hearts; she thrives in Laura's love and gratitude. They enjoy the same mindless videos. She reads the tabloids to Laura, making her smile. With her creativity gone, Laura enjoys hearing people's stories and Hollywood gossip. Gratefully, Laura looks forward to being with her new friend.

Amazingly, Laura is better this week than before December! Today she enjoyed a side-of-bed bath. Her companion helped her wash her hair and encouraged her to eat some yogurt and tiny pieces of apple. Laura asks for cheese and crackers, solid food she hasn't had for over a month. She sleeps deeper with the pain level being less. However, the side effects from the chemical cocktail shut down her bowels and the hourly laxatives give her terrible cramps. But she smiles more. Her eyes have a little sparkle in them. She lives with gratitude, acceptance and grace. She remains ever empathetic to the larger field of human suffering. Without judgement, she tells us who is to be with her, all based on her heart connection to them, to life and to death. Such a wise teacher.

How long can this last? Just when we think she will die, and the hospice team says she is closing down, things turn around. She says she would enjoy one more summer on Colenso. Perhaps she is experiencing 'the surge', a rare burst of good health shortly before death, to say goodbye to life. In this field of death, the mystery penetrates deeper—the transformations, the fluctuations between almost death and not quite life, the ambiguity and mutability of continual uncertainly making it impossible for me to find a stable still point.

When not holding Laura's translucent white hand, I collapse. Somehow John remains connected to a bottomless well of compassion for her, for me and for himself. Grief puts me in a state of self-absorption. I know it is a sanctified time to be in communion with Laura, a time when we dwell so intimately in that other reality—death—yet often I am in a fog of subjective, emotional exhaustion. There is no time for my grief. In silence I witness my body weeping as my heart keeps beating.

John and I are lovers passing in the hallways of Hobbit House. Laura's soul fills her home with loving grace and gratitude, a rare gift for anyone sensitive to such an atmosphere. Her loveliness exemplifies living a life through demonstration. Though bursts of frustration, anger and sadness break through, she quickly re-centers herself when the pain level feels almost tolerable. Melissa comes down on weekends; sits beside her bed and marks English papers. Laura feels comforted by her presence. When Melissa sponge bathes her sister, we hear laughter. The sweet tenderness between them warms my heart and breaks it.

Laura lives an inner security and presence that expresses gratitude rather than polluting the field with negativity. She is an indomitable warrior bringing forth the most positive outcome for all. In life, she was a risk-taker who stretched herself to full capacity, often at the expense of her health. She drank, smoked socially, experimented, and was hungry for the life she loved. And she shone, giving herself completely in love to those who worked with her. She had a way of changing the atmosphere from negative to positive, where her thinking, usually arising from outside the box of conventional thinking, could be heard, received and respected. Even now on her death bed, she breaks the barriers of normalcy. Her soulful beauty transforms darkness into light, her invisible presence leading us through this threshold into death.

Laura continues to teach me about aging, about letting go and dying while remaining alive. Her inner knowing lives boundless love. Yesterday I asked her about it; "I have always found it effortless to love, Mom, even my nemeses." While I fall into emotional drama, she quietly endures each minute. It is effortless to love her. She loves so much and so many love her. She drifts in and out of awareness. In her good moments, Laura communicates with us. I sit beside her bed, my journal open, pen in hand and wait. She speaks of painful realties without attempting to sweeten them up. She speaks truth. Her words are medicine for me to hear. I receive them as they are fully marinated in her love.

"I am embracing death as a new experience. It makes no sense to keep going."

"Oh, darling, you know we would do anything to help you, to fix things, but we can't take your pain away."

"I never asked you to..." she says drifting off. "Sometimes I am swimming in shit and sometimes it is liquid turquoise blue," she sighs and smiles.

"This family blames and shames. Constructive criticism is helpful and wonderful. Blame does nothing but hurt and separate."

After a long silence she opens her eyes.

"I am leaving soon, Mom."

"Where are you going? Leaving for the sunroom, darling, or the planet?"

"Planet. Like the game we played at dinnertime: I am going to the moon, and I will take …remember?" she smiles.

"But I won't be taking anything." Suddenly her eyes open wide in fear. "I am scared."

I give her Ativan. I wait. She calms down into silence.

"What are you scared of, sweetheart? Can you put words to it?"

"What if I can't breathe?"

Her eyes roll up and back. She wills herself to breathe slower and deeper. Such discipline and skill!

Her face softens. "I've signed a document that says you must do what I say."

Closing into the end of January and still she breathes. Sometimes the palliative team tries 'conscious sedation,' but it doesn't work. Through swollen, cracked lips she lets us know she is fully conscious. In this intolerable condition she knows and can't form words; she breathes but can't feel anything; she is alive but dead.

Waking, she whispers: "Tell Melissa I love her. She is right here with me," she smiles, closes her eyes, and drifts off only to repeat the request. She mentions that I must tell John that she loves him. She mentions her friends, naming each one individually, and smiles radiantly when she sees them in her heart. Wordless, we wait, and wait and wait.

Melissa calls daily, wanting to come back, yet after taking so much time off she feels on overdrive with the pressure of teaching. "Oh, Mom, Laura has been dying for so long." Melissa says she will return next weekend and take a leave of absence. The poignancy of sitting with Laura keeps me in the present moment.

"I am going to die tonight, Mom. You don't understand. I am going to die," Laura smiles and closes her eyes. She does not die. All drugs are increased. She loses her sight and all physical strength. She lies perfectly still. I hope she dreams of floating in the water around the island on an air mattress.

On waking she needs to situate herself: "Have I been in an accident?" I tell her she is in her home, Hobbit House. Her skin is pure white except for her swollen legs and football-like feet that now turn slightly purple. Death creeps in. Why prolong this suffering? The palliative team shares our frustration. Doctor-assisted suicide is not yet legal. Controlling pain in the dying is not always possible. Controlling the source of pain is possible; the extreme side effects of the drugs are not.

It is bitterly cold outside, and the sidewalks are icy. "I hate the cold of winter," I say to Melissa as we massage Laura's football feet and legs. Her tissues no longer absorb the saline that keeps her hydrated.

Laura speaks. I put my ear closer to her lips: "I am sorry, Mommy. I too want a warm spring day now. I want to feel the sun on my skin." She delicately cups her hands around my face, "I love you, Mommy".

I go to the kitchen to weep as Melissa rubs cream over Laura's dry skin making her laugh. Dressing her like a child, she puts clean pajamas on her sister. I intuit Melissa feeling torn between her love for Laura and her desire to be home with Erich. I insist she go home, to keep her own life alive. I assure her we will call when it is time.

When one of us leaves, Laura gets agitated. Almost blind now she can't see where she is. Sometimes she lies perfectly still with tears rolling down her face. We sit with her until Steve or one of us arrives. She loves her hospice team whom she has known since September.

When Dr. S takes her hand in his and tenderly asks: "Laura, what is the question you want me to ask today that I have not asked?"

She smiles. Slowly she guides him through her questions as he patiently listens. Laura shares that her body is changing and that she is dying. He bows his head and cries. Always respectful of his nursing team, we know we are blessed with his compassionate care.

13

DYING WITH LAURA

"The physical structure of the universe is love."

–Teilhard de Chardin

February 1

We thought Laura would be dead by the end of January, yet she lives. She says she is awakening as if from a deep sleep. Her dreams of swimming in the Bay, in clear colored water with vast open views of turquoise blue, delight her, making her feel a joyous freedom in an open space. She shares with me she has been given the task of sorting through endless numbers to find the elusive formula of unity, like counting the strands of hair on Rapunzel's head. She looks for new ways of living in the physical world and wants to share it with me. Perhaps her destiny is to grow young again. Hope rises. Did I ever really believe she would die before me? Can I love her without attachment to her living—to her dying? Can I love her enough?

When Laura sleeps, barely breathing beside me, I talk to 'Grandmother Tree'. I ponder if I will sense Laura's Life qualities without her physical body, without feeling her wonderful hugs, without hearing her lyrical voice. How will I endure living when I have lost what I love most—a child, never to be seen or held again? Can I exist without her joyous, fun-loving, wild nature, her deep love of life, her loving kindness?

Everything material slowly slips away from Laura, including her bodily functions.

Through tears today Laura assures me that our mother-daughter love is indestructible.

"I will always visit you, Mom, when you are in silent meditation."

"I will need your help, darling, for my skills are really limited."

"Don't worry, Mommy; I will be there with you."

"Are you sure we can keep in contact?" I ask. She looks into my eyes with complete clarity and answers: "I know, Mom. I know this as fact now."

John shares with me that last night he took a painful journey down memory lane with her. Though her ability to form words is all but gone, he spoke of their trips to auctions, where she playfully gathered an assortment of exotic treasures for Hobbit House. She loved their uniqueness: distinctive lamps, paintings, chairs, music boxes, wine holders, crystals, island stones and little treasures she gathered throughout her life. Laura knew each specific treasure and where she wanted each one to go after she died. It broke John's heart.

The next morning, she tells me she is ready to leave. "I am leaving the planet now and not packing anything."

My feeling of loss is beyond comprehension. I am graced by a sweet form of numbness that allows me to mindlessly function with overflowing love for her. At home on my night off, I find the refrigerator full of food to reheat. I bless our neighbors and friends who silently weep with us, supporting us with acts of love we can't return. No parent should endure the tension of wanting their child to live and wanting their child to die, to end the suffering. Everything I feared when I first heard the diagnosis is now happening—her detachment from her body, her life, the world and all she loved and thrived within. Bit by bit her physical losses are released. Yet, Laura still lives with love.

The image of Mother Mary holding Christ's lifeless body comes to mind. A mother's grief is profoundly spiritual. In the depths of my body, motherlove exists as an all-loving impulse in my flesh. It loves whatever is born, welcoming it back into form from its formless state. The impulse honors the natural world. In essence, real Love knows itself as living spirit animating matter. Matter makes spirit visible throughout its cellular nature. Patriarchal culture buried real love, yet it still lives inside my bone marrow. Where are the stories of Mary's journey of loss, the mother whose crucified son is the focus of the Christian story? Is this the experience of Mary, Mother of Christ, with her crucified son on her lap? Why does no one focus on the quality of her loss, her motherlove? Is the trinity of mother-daughter-holy spirit less than the father-son-holy spirit? Are they all part of the same phenomena? The bleeding heart, the intersection of life and death, the symbol of the cross, motherlove—one day I might understand."

I cannot suffer another's pain, even my beloved Laura's. Perhaps that is what I find hardest to endure.

I want to take her pain, make it mine, so she can live a full and radiant life. I hover in a condition that is neither alive nor dead, simply here, now, holding her hand in mine. When sadness breaks through her bone-body I can't control living or dying. I cry with her tears. I collapse with her in defeat. Gently I lean over her to whisper in her ear, "I love you, darling Laura. I love you, my darling." Tears roll down her cheeks. We wait for her next breath. In silence, I commune with 'Grandmother Tree':

"Will she live?"

"No."

"Was she ever born?"

"No and yes."

"Will she stay with us?"

"Always. She will leave the door open for anyone who has the eyes to see. She builds the bridge now."

"The rainbow bridge I saw in meditation after her premature birth?"

"Yes, even as she sleeps, she works."

I feel an impulse in my belly.

"She works on dying, Mary, on the freedom of being alive in space, of being aware in the formless field of Love—complete, full and nothing."

"But on this side of life. How do I see her in death?"

"One IS. Let the vehicle do what you have been trained to do. You have a voice now."

"Who will listen?"

"You and whoever needs to hear. They will find you. Keep being and writing."

"Do miracles happen?"

"LIFE *is* the miracle."

"Is this the voice of old Nellie, the crone who spoke to me after Christopher's stillbirth?

"You have always been her. Shift identities."

"Is Nellie the being, imagining me in a form with a human voice?"

"Yes."

"Am I the being, imagining the hand that writes, the mind that records, the body that senses, the mother who grieves? "

"Yes."

"Did I work with Buddha?"

"Yes, and now you work with the Christ impulse. Allow being to experience itself as physical matter, with sensory perception. Being transforms pain and suffering into freedom and great love."

"And what is this freedom?"

"You know this already: freedom from collective thinking, freedom from your unconscious attachments to flesh, flesh held in bondage of concretized self-images."

"Do I transcend the body?"

"No! Be flesh, free of mental attachments to its form. Then you are free to be of the substance of Love. Every healthy cell in your body knows this."

"Original flesh?"

"Yes. You wrote that. Death teaches you to die before your physical death."

Shifting focus, I notice the slow rise and fall of Laura's breathing. Her destiny is to die in pain: mine is to suffer the awareness of death, stay present and conscious. I discern the difference between self-absorption with my own suffering and moments of impersonal experience of being one-with Laura. Within my physical nature, I experience an expansion into a larger sense of self. Devoid of personal suffering, I abide in an 'ocean of selfless-love'. Dying with Laura, I too die to my history from birth to now, releasing ego identities and self-images. Together, whatever is left, is made aware of another way of knowing that is intimately realized—made real. Here, we resonate with the same surrounding sound that acknowledges fundamental truths. Our stable, predictable selves, existing as separate people, awaken. Free of time-bound thinking, we are one in the threshold of eternal communion.

I sense subtle changes; things seem connected, joined, glued together in love. Deep impulses lengthen into arms that wrap around our individual reality. The boundaries holding the holes within my heart soften, relax their fearful grasp. I sense myself relaxing and expanding into an all-loving atmosphere. I am free of suffering. I am whole and experience a certainty that all is as it should be—even when my head tells me something is very wrong, and Laura is dying.

Dwelling in this silent field, I am created. I do not re-create myself into an image. My mind creates self-images, but I am not a mental image—I am existence, acutely aware of being one-with Laura. This realization reverses my thinking—I possess nothing. How can I own a life, a daughter, my body? Now, in this timeless dimension of consciousness, we belong to a vast field of loving light. In this moment, in this particular form, I uniquely express loving light—it lives me so I become IT. I am the love that the blind see, and the deaf hear. I awaken inside a dynamic truth that still resides deep, down inside me. This reality lives me, breathes me, and creates me. It is all that I AM. I am dying inside an eternal I AM, the Divine Mother Womb of earth, of matter, of unobstructed Love. Centered in my head with my eyes looking out, I perceive discrete objects. Centered, field-wise within my heart, I apprehend unconditional Love for all Life on Planet Earth. Centered in my belly, I sense the Divine Motherlove pulsing within every perceivable cell in me and everything around me in Hobbit House. Every physical cell uniquely is pulsed by this Love. The pulse of Love, the catalyst animating planetary forms, creates each form to uniquely sound a specific aspect of its Loving Truth.

I leave a love note on our bed for John to read on his next night at home:

"Darling: These next weeks will not be easy. Love never dies though all things born die. Love dwells in the unborn and lives through the bodies it forms, to express its Life. Our darling Laura lives this and has all her life. You do as well, my darling, and I am learning still. Learning what? To Be the Love we are in the first place, the Love that never dies, the Love permeating all things and never separates into isolated parts at birth. It will be this Love that sustains us these next weeks. It will transport our darling Laura Home— home to the whole so she is always us, always in LIFE and within all manifesting forms."

With this glimmering insight, I am able to sit on a rim of invisible life inside physical forms and be with my dying daughter. Love lives—love for Laura; for me, her mother; for John, her father; for Melissa, her sister, and for Laura's many friends. Without thought, I know how to live: I roll out of bed, put my feet on the floor. "Something will happen today. I have no idea what. Show up and I will know what I need to do." What I once labelled 'robot fog' transforms into effortless living—a mother in deep grief. I dwell in a soft subterranean field of velvet darkness, of boundless intimacy embracing physical exhaustion and profound sorrow. I live in a community with all the parents who hold their dying child in their arms. I connect to humanity in death: we all die. However, when I have the courage to love so deeply that my boundaries of self dissolve, I still suffer and know Real Love for the first time.

Holding Laura's hand in mine, I stare at her family ring, now on my finger as hers are too thin.

Her blurry eyes try to open. She asks:

"Who am I?"

"You are Laura Christina Hamilton, darling, and you are in your own home."

More silence. I speak to her with my inner voice:

"Why can't you die?"

Immediately I hear her voice, vital and strong inside me. She answers.

"It is not in the stars."

"Are you meant to live?"

"Yes."

"So you won't die?"

"No. Mom, wake up! The 'I' who you commune with now was never born and I am the Laura-child you have loved, the Laura person. We had what was an ordinary mother-daughter relationship with all its loves and struggles. It was you-me; now we are One in the field of loving light. Remember the Whole and the hole, the W/hole where we lived and live now and always will?"

"What do you want to say to me, darling?"

"Nothing you don't already know. Stop projecting. Wake up! At source we are not persons. No me and no you. You have too many opinions, Mom. Drop them and know."

The image of the Mother Mary re-appears. Did she know the profound wisdom revealed in suffering and death when archetypes are reversed? When her son was dying, did he share communion in the luminous ground, both flesh and fleshless? Did she realize Christ as the resurrected One because she was living the same resurrected body, still born of flesh? Is this motherlove? Has humanity focused on the suffering of the male deity to the exclusion of the mother-love instinct, alive and deep within the eternal womb-wisdom of planetary Life—in the living womb of all women?

Laura's breathing pattern changes. Silent tears roll down her face. Through swollen lips I pick up her words. She mourns for all that she loves and has lost: the beauty of the island, the feeling of heat from the sun on her body, the sense of coolness when swimming, her wonderful job, her friends, the taste of wine, the feeling of a good poop, chewing, tasting food, swallowing effortlessly, seeing where she is. A deep breath of realization breathes us. Her loss is complete.

Is this attachment to things or Love for invisible Divine Life intimately present inside all things? Is it possible to love without a desire to possess, to be free of clinging without fear of loss, 'to kiss the joy as it flies' (Blake). Did Laura experience the wondrous joy of Life in the flesh, its natural goodness? Did she have the heart-eye to see into the sacred nature of things? Is this the wisdom of suffering into physical death—to awaken to Divine Life, 'to kiss the grief as it flies'?

Laura drifts off, the slow rise and fall of her chest reveals she is peaceful. In stillness, she endures the bedsores inching into her bones. Beside her, I breathe with Grandmother Tree. Her naked branches reach toward the winter sun, waiting, waiting for the warming light of spring to soften the frozen earth. Are the newly born leaves alive inside her branches pushing their way outwards to open into daylight? I have no hope—but—I trust spring will arrive. The eternal nature of the LIFE force behind seasonal change continues to emit impulses. Birth into form guarantees death will follow. The force that brings birth also changes all things into rotting compost, where worms transform dying matter into rich nutrients, creating nourishment for new life waiting to be born. Again and again, season after season, spring arrives freshly new, and, when the flow reverses, winter arrives, freshly new—death, a new season. The thread of Life continues through the whole and the hole appears and dissolves.

John and I now sleep upstairs together in Hobbit House. In the middle of the night the nurse calls to us: "Laura needs to talk to you both."

"I think I died, but I decided to come back. May I have something to drink, please?"

I give her a lemon swab to suck on.

John: "Where were you?" She smiles, eyes still closed. "I'll explain a little later." We wait in silence.

"I just met God," she mumbles, smiling knowingly. "I want people to know you can die and come back. I know. I just did it."

She drifts off. We wait.

"I died you know and came back."

"Why did you come back, darling?" I ask.

"It wasn't time."

She drifts off again.

"WOW," she mumbles through her swollen, smiling lips.

"How was it being dead?"

"Extraordinary."

"Can you describe it?"

"No words for it."

"What of colors, shapes, movements?"

"Inside lighting—electric blue. Not right word. Everything was it. Real like the rocks."

"And your pain?"

"Pain free, floating inside a warm bath, held by the sky."

"And coming back?"

"Agony."

"So why return?"

"Not my time yet. I am embracing death as a new experience in life."

Laura's beauty radiates through her bone body that speaks of starvation, pain, and drugs. Everything in the room shimmers, including beloved Laura. In our powerlessness to help her live, we witness a sacred presence that keeps Laura breathing and Grandmother Tree rooted in the frozen earth. We wait in silence, mere points of stillness sitting in stark beauty, experiencing existence in the face of nonexistence.

14

DEATH'S SPACE

"Our normal waking consciousness, rational consciousness as we call it, is but one special type of consciousness, whilst all about it, parted from it by the filmiest of screens, there lie potential forms of consciousness entirely different."

–William James (The Varieties of Religious Experience**)**

March 1, 2014

I recognize in Laura's bones, the ancient woman I met when I first looked at her in the incubator. Her premature birth taught me I couldn't control life. Ross Woodman translated my experience into his poem "Old woman grow young again". We taped a haiku poem to her incubator: "Holding her close so she looks bigger than she is/ summer rose." Holding her soft, perfect body had overwhelmed me with inexpressible love. My mind knew I loved 'my baby,' while my body lived the wisdom of motherlove in service of Life. At the time,

I couldn't sense this wisdom. I was too terrified she would die. I had already known what it was to love a dead baby. My task following Laura's birth was to love her regardless if she lived or died. She lived.

Laura's loving presence for the past 35 years has been a gift. Now, her death teaches me of my attachment to her as 'my daughter'. Without the sense of possessiveness, I feel the privilege of her being in our lives. Her life and her death are gifts not asked for yet given. Like Laura, I drift in and out of time and timelessness. When in timelessness, I live deep peace. The familiar sense of me, the doer who tries to make things better, now lives in an unsolvable situation. There is nothing to do but wait and not go unconscious. I hear the words, 'Real Love never separates,' but the living reality of Laura dying and functioning as a parent is radically different! Will I be able to love her enough?

Everything in my mother-body wants to nurse her back to life. Attuning to a larger field of substantiating Love, I realize the sacred mother-love instinct is buried deeply in the wilderness background of my awareness. It lives W/holy Love and embraces me now. In death space, personal motherlove transforms into a portal that opens into a background experience. Here, Great Mother Love, the instinct living me now, makes it possible to endure the agony of a breaking heart. I realize there are many aspects of embodied life that share the temple of this human flesh I now am.

Meditating in Laura's room, the silence speaks. In my journal I write:

"Just keep writing. Focus elsewhere, beyond your little i-suffering. Open the eye of your heart. Be free of the bondage of collective images, sealed inside the limits of form. The sensitivity of flesh functions as a finely tuned receptor capable of detecting impulses way beyond the physical self. Living flesh, free of limiting self-images of a separate body, will register impulses inside space as well as outside space. Space is always space. Allow silent attention to open into experience that lives presence beyond your skull, beneath the soles of your feet, your heart and beyond the boundaries of every organ in your body. In that space real freedom abides. Who is creating you now? Who do you think is living now, holding this pen— your ego subjective self or a mystery that you do not see with your physical eye?"

Perhaps the secret of our mother-daughter relationship is held in the spontaneous vision of a rainbow bridge that appeared the first night of Laura's life. There was no guarantee that she would live. Securely anchored in my heart, the Rainbow extended into her wee body, pulsed LIFE into her physical body, taking root in her heart and now opens into the invisible sensate reality alive in death's space.

Laura shares with me that she dreams of all the people she knows. "They all wear T-shirts with a cool camp logo, 'Beaver Canoe'. I am confused. I don't know if I am at camp or at the island. Am I at your home or Hobbit House? I think I am in a prison. It's hard to put it together, Mom. It is scary when it's a prison. I don't know what I did and then I don't know who I am or where I am. Then I go into this space that's the color of blue inside flashes of lightning."

"What happens there, darling?"

"Nothing, I just am, but it's so good because at least I know where I am and who I am. The whole world doesn't make any sense. The lightning blue feels so loving. No people there, for we are all part of this light. It's harmonic, peaceful. I spend a lot of my time there now. When I am not there I get worried and feel I must get things figured out or go back to prison."

"Is prison your body, Laura?"

"I'm not sure. I am sure of the love you guys have for me and me for you. I am sure about love in general."

"Does love have a color, a shape?"

"No, it's just everywhere. It's weird. Everything is weird. Geometry becomes literature and then math becomes grammar. It's all the same. If I were an artist, I could draw it. I will try and write. I just wish I had a normal schedule."

March 1

"I can't find the exit sign. I want to go. I want to be free and play again," she smiles.

Long silence.

"I can be with you guys all the time. I am so tired of being stuck here, in pain. I want to go now." She falls into a deep rhythmic breathing pattern. The next morning Melissa arrives on a three-week leave. On waking and finding Melissa beside her, Laura smiles. I witness the poignant tenderness between them. The palliative team arrives. She asks to die. We learn the full-body seizures she has had for the last few weeks are a side effect from the pain medications.

Gently, Dr. S whispers to her: "I will give you something to help find the exit sign, Laura." In gratitude, she smiles and whispers, "Thank you."

We wait.

Laura asks us who she is. She hears us but can't remember her name. She can't see her familiar surroundings.

"Lovely Laura, darling Laura," we repeat and repeat, and each time she thanks us. In tears, her PSW companion for the last month tells her she loves her. Laura, smiling, nods her head slightly in acknowledgement. We are told not to let her drink anything; her swallowing function will go soon. When she asks for water, all we can give her are swabs soaked in lemon water. Nothing touches her thirst caused by the drugs.

A night nurse arrives; but she doesn't read the new instructions left by the palliative team. Feeling compassion for Laura, she gives her two large glasses of water. Laura rallies the next morning. I see her cut lip is already healing from her fall the other night. Her young body still functions. How can her body both die and heal? The pharmacist calls, concerned about the amount of morphine and repeats, 'it's enough to kill an elephant'.

I watch Steve tenderly stroke her arm as he talks to her. I watch Melissa give her injections in her hollowed stomach. I witness the tears running down John's face as he leans over her to hear his beloved daughter trying to tell him something.

Refocus…breathe. Need to go home tonight to do her laundry. In the car I hear myself screaming, "I am insane, berserk with unbearable grief!" I hear a voice whisper, "Just push the gas pedal to the floor and it will all be over, Mary. You don't need to suffer anymore." At the stop sign at the end of our street, I linger, pausing, waiting for my foot to press the gas pedal to the floor, to put an end to it.

An invisible force bangs me over the head. A demanding voice screams out of my heart. "No Mary! Don't be so selfish. Wake up and realize what your suicide would do to John, Melissa and to Laura!"

I return to my senses. Suicide is not an answer to end this intolerable grief. I realize how gently Laura's loved ones walk in unison, in grace. We are one in her death, dying with her in our own way, while we live with her in Hobbit House. Night nurses come and go. Her PSW arrives faithfully, reminding us of the pill schedule as she cleans and tidies Hobbit House. The palliative team comes twice a day. We wait.

Laura's energy begins to shift. The vitality that was once in her begins to lift outside her. Her focus has shifted away from life. She will die soon. Erich arrives to support Melissa. We cry when alone and function tenderly during our four-hour shifts with Laura. Throughout the days and nights, one of us sits by her bed, holding her hand.

Sometimes when I sit with Laura, my energy expands out of me. A silver string connects my solar plexus with an awareness soaring through other dimensions. I am huge with Life, not huge as body, but as limitless space. Is Laura taking me with her? Is she building the Rainbow Bridge linking our hearts in subtle dimensions I am not aware of? No matter how many tears I cry and no matter how heavy I am with grief, I am also aware of a growing lightness.

I no longer feel the polarities of life and death pulling me apart. The opposites collapse in and down, and a single point of awareness rises into my heart and stabilizes—a symbol of a crystal rose. I am alive and dead. Laura too, is alive and dying. Her bones remain, rising and falling with each slow breath, yet all she was in this life has gone. The rippling bed makes it appear as if she is moving herself. I breathe with her. Inhaling anchors the reality of suffering;

exhaling releases me into a spherical being of light. Between hitting rock bottom and open space, between up and down, in and out, life and death, weighted and weightless, I am lived as I die with Laura. Why is her heart still beating? No why. Life is. Stay awake.

In 1990, I wrote in the book, *Leaving My Father's House*: "The point is to die before you are dead, to have no one home and know it." Now it carries deeper significance. I witness thoughts floating by. No clinging. No wanting. No hoping. Breathing— dying with Laura. Living in flesh. I write:

"Laura dies in her bed. The unborn beauty inside her flesh begins to live now as universal love, the love she is and always was—the real Love alive within the darkness sealed inside discrete forms."

I linger on the edge of an unseen world; death's horizon approaches, but the precipice keeps moving away. In complete vulnerability and purity of her love, Laura lies serenely as the rippling mattress rises and falls. Young and ancient, living while dying in beauty, I wait…and wait…

Dr. S arrives. Taking her hand from mine, he sits with her silently. She does not respond to his gentle questions, yet softly smiles. She recognizes his touch.

"Is it time, Laura? Is today the day to die?"

No response. We wait in the other room. Eventually he joins us, "We can turn off the oxygen and see what happens. Some people die instantly, others linger."

We agree it is time. The low hum of Darth Vapor, the oxygen machine that we have lived with since the island, stops. Silence. Nothing happens. We listen to her breathing. There are long pauses between each inhale as she lingers between life and death.

We continue to take four-hour shifts with Laura. After 24 hours she continues to breathe in deep, rhythmic slow breaths, bridging differing realities. The palliative nurses report that all her vital systems are holding strong. We take turns going to the market to pick up food for the living.

For three days we drink from the river of death. Swells of grief and love absorb me with an emptiness of thought. Holding her white porcelain hand in my wrinkled, sun spotted one, an unfamiliar clarity arises—discrete forms appear and fall into nothingness. Separations dissolve: life–death, Laura-me, sacred-profane, spirit-matter, here-there, nothing-everything, empty-full. A new atmosphere effortlessly births itself, remains nameless, invading everything in silent, tender existence.

On the third morning I go home early to launder Laura's sheets. Suddenly I know I must urgently return to Hobbit House. John sits beside her bed, caressing her hand. I see his exhausted sadness. She remains the same. I take her hand at noon. At 12:30 her breathing grows stronger, deeper, as if she is giving birth. I call out: "She is leaving us." Melissa and John circle her bed. Five deep cleansing breaths, then stillness... silence.

I watch the cloud of white vapor circle around her heart and leave. The shapeless vapor that lived her and shaped her life lingers around her upper body. In the background I hear Erich phoning Steve to return. Quietly, John leaves the room to call the palliative team to sign the death certificate.

With warm water scented with sacred oil, Melissa and I bathe our beloved Laura.

For months I have not be able to hold her in my arms, as her pain was too great. Melissa supports her head of dark curly hair on her shoulder. Tenderly we move and cleanse her warm body and dress her in her favorite 'moose flannelette pajamas' and camp director's sweatshirt. Steve slips on her delicate earrings, the barn swallow ones that she loved, and that he gave her. John places the small wooden urn with Tim's ashes in her hands to rest on her heart, just as she asked him to. She is peaceful and utterly beautiful.

I go upstairs to her meditation room to weep as Steve takes his final leave with her body. I sit in her chair with my tears falling on a blank page of my journal. She immediately starts talking to me.

"I am here, Mommy. You are so wrong in some of your views."

"Will you help to correct my perception, or adjust it?"

"I am doing that now. Just relax and be, like Martin. I work like him now, pure play, so easy."

"Are you free of suffering, Laura?"

"Completely."

"Will you continue to speak to me?"

"Always."

"Guide me?"

"If you will listen. You are rather opinionated and closed down."

"Yes, darling, I am. Life isn't always easy."

"It can be, Mom. You have to re-adjust your sight."

"Are you content?"

"Very."

"Is Tim there?"

"Your thoughts, Mom, not mine."

"You're everywhere, aren't you?"

"Yes."

Her familiar presence fills Hobbit House. We are held in a 'warm bath of electric blue, inside lightning'. We take turns sitting with her as her beloved body cools. We touch her, blessing her body with our kisses.

By dinner time we decide it is time for her to go. As planned over a month ago, John calls the Simple Alternative staff to come. They arrive in an unmarked large station wagon. With great respect they enter Hobbit House. We wait in the living room until they appear with darling Laura inside a body bag. We stand, silently place our hands on her body and pause, blessing all she was and is and will be.

John and I watch the men slip the blue bag carrying our daughter into the back of the station wagon. Holding hands in silence we watch from her front room as they drive away. We are stung with indigestible grief.

15

THRESHOLD OF ETERNAL COMMUNION

"True communication is communion—the realization of the oneness, which is love."

—Eckhart Tolle

March 5, 2014

Our devoted neighbors deliver a hot dinner. We eat for the first time without Laura's special breathing bed sounding like ocean swells in the back room. Without past and without future, we dwell in the present. We find we can't leave her home or leave her loving presence. Lying in her upstairs bed, with Melissa and Erich in her basement apartment and Steve back in his home, a familiar joyousness consumes me. Laura's presence lives inside her Hobbit home and inside me. I think of Steve alone and instantly I smile, "I am inside everything now, Mom."

Two days later my beloved daughter's body goes into the fire of cremation. I sit in her meditation chair with my open journal. The winter sun streams through the picture window, warming me and nourishing Laura's vibrant indoor plants. I write:

"I sit on the threshold of form and the formless, the space where solid forms lose their shape and transform into invisible Life. My physical brain won't function here, yet, abiding inside it, I intuit existence. I linger in this spaciousness; the fear of the unknown arises. The familiar impulse to contract back into my familiar self to stay safe isn't present. There is nothing to identify with, to cling to and even to know. What lives when patterns of fear don't exist? Must I release my identification as Laura's mother? How could I forget the joy she brought to me? Wake up! Her loving, joyous nature cannot die."

I hit rock bottom in the knowledge that the body I loved as Laura, is turning into ash. I endure the loss, the yawning ache expands and the reality of physical life disintegrates—I am not rebounding as in other situations I have endured before. I do not want to turn back to my life of the living. I descend deeper and deeper, as if there is a great hole in the bottom of the well of mother-grief, as if there is a hole in my physical being that will not heal. An unfamiliar sense of density textures itself inside the hole where there is nothing to grasp, nothing to find and nothing for a drowning mother to cling to. What felt like sky above and bedrock below evaporate into an opening field of awareness. I am nothing—no image, no thinking, no feeling—only a sound of sobbing, only the feeling of hot tears and snot oozing. I know nothing, feel like nothing, yet I am awake. A silent space opens into a vast, living, unbound field with no visible horizon. Whatever grows here has different roots to tether it to another reality. I am that nameless one inside an unknown reality. The weeping mother's body is all part of this nameless awakening. Telepathically Laura and I commune:

"Mom, do not love me as I was. Love me as I AM."

"Does this require I die with you, darling?"

"Go with it, Mom. Die and be born here now, forever here. "

"And how would you explain here, Laura?"

"It's everywhere, like the H2o of water…can't separate the parts and still have water. It's the secret igniting everything, everywhere—you there, me here—same and different. Go deeper, so deep, you know because you ARE."

"Are what?"

"Everything! Then everything will delight you and you will know you know nothing but awareness itself and that's okay. Just learn to die. At the end of each breath, die again and again and, one day, when you are fully dead—dead to all that you have learned and everything you think you know—then the *real* you will begin to smile in you."

"Why smile?"

"You die into the real, Mom, the knowing… the Flame. Die without resistance. Another form of awareness will arise with other eyes—a single, open spirit eye of transparency. Conventional reality can't function here; you will realize this in your physical ego brain-body. Eye and your physical nature grow in the same soul-soil, share the same life space—inside the same locale where sacred energies endlessly dance in confluent play."

"How can that be?"

"You already are it, the ONE, the secret ONE that is ALL. You're inside that, outside that and a particle of that. Once known, you will live a life of demonstration. No need for a lot of words—just Be what you already are—here, now and always."

I look at the clock. Her body burns in roaring flames…Oh, my beautiful Laura!

"Mom, the worst that can happen to you has happened. I died of cancer. Let go of your attachment to me and to things. Let the tic toc time flow through you. It is all in the placement of awareness, of the spiritual eye, the still point, the fulcrum at the center between all that is. You know this, the deep-sighted eye that apprehends from the depths into the depths. Mom, when you dwell here, we are free. We naturally help all things that suffer. Please Mommy, me on this side, you on that side, both in the indivisible eye of spirit— fiercely—fearlessly—free beyond all conventions, all expectations, illusions, agendas, imagination…and OF LOVE—you of the Love that's created in flesh: me of fleshless Love. Same Love."

"How?"

"No how—live IT…in me, with me, now the ONE."

"But why us, Laura?"

"No why. No cause. Life is as it is. Become w/holy."

Silence. I have no idea what to do. I feel my

body rocking back and forth, keening and weeping. I want Laura alive. Will these words ever make sense? I hear her voice inside me:

"Love never loses itself, Mom. It is the invisible lightning that in a flash of insight changes everything. It is the atmosphere that permeates the quality of your physical body, transforming the unbearable into bearable lightness bursting into bloom again… and again… and again. Love shapes everything into form and then lives through the form. Personal love separates what it loves and attaches to it as a possession; then it clings to it in fear of losing it. And when it is lost, great suffering happens. Love is. It never changes, yet it constantly creates changes in physical life. It shifts atmospheres, temperature, light and weight. It loves all that exists, the whole and the hole where human eyes can't see…and it lives you now. It permeates everything.

"Your suffering binds you, Mom, to the past. Release your clinging nature and allow Love to gather what remains. Be mutable—freshly born— still born in the territory of the unconditioned soul. She is the one who never left her original land of spirit, the one who remembers her arrival, the unique creation born of source. Be the awareness of source inside the physical."

Laura's plants delight in the fresh winter air coming through a tiny space in the open window. They joyously sing in the sun, their beauty radiating in all directions, as if they have tiny inner suns shining inside their greenness. Everything dissolves into sameness—Life delightfully creating itSelf into a myriad of shapes without ever losing its true nature.

The fire consumes Laura's beloved flesh, flesh created with the Life blood in my body. Fire, flame, sun, lava—same source, same properties—flesh to ashes, motherlove to spiritual wine. Who I was as Laura's mother now swims in the deep waters of grief and loss. Yet, I also write from inside the flame that burns up self-images of me and my grief. Inside the flame, beneath the weight of personal suffering, spaciousness opens, unveiling what exists now, eternally here, both seen and unseen.

Mother-heart knows the beauty and value of living flesh that pulses within cycles of dying and forever becoming. The quality of this tenderness unwearyingly embraces world suffering in silence, as the womb encloses the fetus in a woman's body.

Yet, the female body has been idolized in unrealistic images, devalued and demonized by religious dogma and sacrificed to serve idealized spirit. Still Born, flesh and fleshless, the spiritual eye reflects in the mirror of forms, a physical reality spontaneously bursting forth from inside itself, revealing the beauty of Spirit Life.

I am heavy with sorrow. I sit in the heavy. I hear my body weep. All is blackness; a void without content... nothing... a tiny light appears...a star? It brings a focal point in the midnight sky of blackness. Don't think. Don't create. Accept, allow, observe and BE what is. No effort. No imagination.

A wee little bird looks at me in the window, fluttering its wings like a hummingbird. But it is winter and hummingbirds are down South and there are no flowers, yet the bird reappears. Oh, such sweetness!

Laura's thin bone-body is now ashes. The titanium hip retracted to be recycled for someone else to walk again. Her suffering ends; the silence within my breathing coalesces into a ruby red crystal. Waves of memories of the fullness of her life are searing flames of grief. She is forever gone, yet her distinctive footprint of Love presses forever deeper into my heart and seeps into this mother-flesh. We are one.

I hear myself cry out to her: "Darling Laura, remember your name, the sound of your Laura-home, so when I call you, you will be here. I beg you not to leave me."

"Mom, only you can sever the connection between us. I can't, for I am All, loving everything, joyously complete in itSelf."

"Oh, Laura, please remember this and don't close the gap in your next incarnation. Remember your birth!"

"Good advice for yourself, Mom. I will teach you to be a Being in flesh as you taught me to be a person in flesh. You are now 'my love'. I am timeless. What a relief."

"Agonized relief, darling."

"Oh, stop the drama and drop the agonizing. Agonizing is your grief for you to deal with. My suffering is over. Now you suffer for yourself."

"Awkward for me in public."

"Absolutely, Mom. Love awkward; there will be plenty of it in your life now."

"I love you, darling Laura…always…."

I step into a future without beloved Laura in my human life. I can't stop crying. Grief absorbs me. I am both dying with her and living with her. The memories of her final breath linger in my soul. Oh, how I loved her body, her beautiful form, her dark curly hair, her arms around me, her laughter, her joy in being alive, her engaging smile...

"Stay with me as I am, Mom, not as I was. Then, we can work together. I work on this side, you on that side. Together we build the bridge, the rainbow bridge, inward to the One."

16

LIFE AFTER DEATH

"What is essential is invisible to the eye."

–Antoine De Saint-Exupery

March 6, 2014

We can't leave Hobbit House. We are too raw to go home, and Laura's joy fills the atmosphere of her home as if to comfort us, reassure us that all is well, when it feels so awful. Without any idea what to do and no one to ask, I sit in her mediation room surrounded by her vibrant green plants and soak in the warming winter sun with them. I mourn my loss: the fetus who grew under my heart; the baby who nursed at my breast; the child I raised; the teenager who drove me nuts and simultaneously loved; the professional woman I admired and respected; the adult who taught me about grief when her beloved Tim died; the daughter who broke my heart when she died. I ponder what skills to practice to find the invisible being of Laura. How will I recognize nothing as something? She returns to source…meaningless words when my lifeblood weeps, and grief eats the marrow of my bones. Is freedom from this personal suffering released in dying? And, does dying while still born require that I see my attachments, disengage from identifications as a separate person and become real again as something other? Is everything invisibly connected? Is a rainbow bridge that I experienced at her premature birth gathering substance? Will I become unbound, uprooted and crazy…or will roots grow into an impersonal realm where trees commune and rocks are alive? How will I get through her Tribute? All those people! Keep breathing…

Ten days later, we walk into the huge Convention center. It is packed despite it being March Break Holiday, and severe snow squalls threaten safety on the roads. Laura's friends from the Y transform a cold impersonal conference room into a beautiful Laura space. It feels like a cathedral, perfumed with trumpet white lilies and large encased candles. The soft lighting draws attention to a huge screen just to the side of the speaker's platform. Laura's radiant smile and sparkling eyes fill the screen, bringing light to the heavy space. Throughout the afternoon, a slideshow runs, professionally created by the Y's media team. Everyone pitched in. Everyone loves her.

Holding hands tightly, John and I walk to the front row and sit in two empty seats. Without hearing, we listen to the program we designed—first Melissa speaks, then Laura's three oldest friends, the Never Wives Club, recount through tears and laughter, hilarious stories of growing up with Laura. Her cousins and special friends read Laura's Roary stories. Her Photoshop photos, that accompany Roary's rhymes in the stories, appear on the screen. The program ends with the only words I hear: "Laura didn't die."

Psychic friends tell me Laura touches into the hearts of anyone who sees or feels her presence. I hear her whispering in my heart: "I'm here, Mom; I'm here." Beloved camp friends sing the heart-felt songs she loved. Sometimes I glance briefly at the screen and see pictures I have not seen of her with campers, camp friends and school friends. Between each photo a poetic phrase appears, expressing seeds of inspiration she planted in her various friends and little campers that changed the direction of their lives. I can't look at the screen and cope. I turn my back to it and greet people. It is 'awkward' for them and for me, yet Laura's radiant smile spreads through our hearts. Laura is everywhere, and her body is not here. She can't die because this great Love is here, is everywhere. We feel it, know it, for we are living it, participating inside the love along with her. Is this the resurrected body, alive within and without everything? Am I dying and living with her—in Her?

I see myself in the black wool dress, the moth holes newly stitched invisibly by a beloved friend. My body freezes: "No need for you to talk, Mom. Awkward! Hold silence. Enjoy it." Her voice relaxes me, transforming tension into melting love. I remember her saying to me years ago, "Love comes so easily to me, Mom. It is effortless. I never have to try. It's just there." No wonder she is loved by so many.

Three weeks later we sell Hobbit House. We give her treasures to her grieving friends. John encourages me to teach a workshop in South Carolina where it is warm. With nothing else planned, I find myself with my carry-on suitcase, in buses, airports, planes, taxis, and end up in a beautiful conference center. I open my suitcase to unpack and realize I brought all the conference teaching materials I need, but nothing personal. Always, when I am facilitating psychological dream and deep body work, I bring family photos to keep me connected to the joys of my life. Stunned, I recognize my work clothes in the suitcase and wonder who I am. I teach, listen, hear dreams and empathize with pain-filled stories causing deep trauma. Through the week I recite poetry, remember conference details and select the appropriate music for various exercises. I hear the resonance in my voice, deep, full and present, moment by moment. With the past too raw, the future too unknown, alertness keeps me focused in the moment driven by my fear of disintegrating.

May-June 2014

The winter ice melts in early May. We return to our soul-home with Melissa, Erich, and Steve to scatter Laura's ashes. Silently, in single file we walk the island path to Noggin's Lagoon, Laura's favorite place for early morning and bedtime skinny dips. Holding her bronze urn next to his heart, John silently leads the way. We take turns scattering her ashes around the sprouting flowers, the rocks and the water at Noggin's. Our bodies exhausted, our minds thick with grief, we silently return to the cottage.

Life continues without our darling Laura. Through grace we endure the unbearable personal loss held in the unbreakable invisible bond of Boundless Love.

Life dances us forward into the next step when everything within us wants to move backwards to the days when Laura's joy and laughter permeated our world. The daily experience of her absence creates a vast stillness, a great open space, a void of raw nothingness. My physical body mourns with despair. Never again will I feel her wonderful hugs. Never again will I hear her voice. My animal body folds in upon itself. My soul's voice whispers: "Keep breathing."

Daily I go to the small studio-cabin that we call the Hermitage, a quiet place for grieving, meditating and alone time. Looking out at the open view, I hear the words Laura whispered into my heart during her cremation. "Love me as I am, Mom, not as I was."

"So you are not dead, my darling?"

"Bodiless, yes. Still here, not born in flesh. You are still born, Mom. Live your existence in fullness. I did. Still living, only now I live inside all Life and still fully conscious."

"Are you the resurrected body?"

"Call it what you want, Mom. I am here now with you, and you know it. Flesh or fleshless, temporary or eternal, you in body, me not in body and here. Same."

"And so different! I know those are labels, darling. I know words construct conventional reality. But how do I know you are here? How do I know that you are not in my imagination to make me feel better? Am I reconstructing the image of you from the qualities you lived in life and now project them into a being of light without a physical form?"

"Mom, I don't speak words. I AM Life."

"But I want you, Laura. I want your body, your flesh, your blood, your bone reality. I want to see and feel your hair, hear your laughter, pick up the phone and recognize your voice. I want you, Laura."

Tears stream down my face.

"Want what you like, Mom. It doesn't change the fact that I am here. Be what you know, without words, without concepts, without labels. It's all here. Dead or alive, stillborn, still born, not born, always here."

"But I need things. I need you, not some idea or ghost voice."

"Always a thing to you, Mom. To me? Still here. No big difference. I am not an idea, and you know this. I am neither a ghost nor a concept of a dead person. Go beyond all that. Go beyond your thinking."

"But I will fall apart. I won't know who I am."

"See Mom, I know your thoughts before you do. You won't lose your flesh, your opinions and your ideas. Don't worry; they will all be there, floating around the surface of your brain creating your reality—a pretty fragile reality. Brain doesn't shape my being here, and death doesn't stop my being here either."

I sense I am being opened into a rarefied atmosphere very different from earth's reality. I hear my physical body keening with grief. I feel inner impulses pushing and pulling me, rocking me gently back and forth to the rhythmic lullaby of breath with my snot flowing. I comprehend that I am an expression of world sorrow, an utter grief in the marrow of my bones. It is not pretty; it destroys all conceptual thinking; it annihilates my sense of self—but—it is Real. Rock-bottom truth—we die— no personal self left so what still lives?

I feel myself relaxing, as if slipping into a warm bath on a cold winter night. My spine naturally unwinds. I pause in soundless meditation, stunned after the physical exertion of expressing a bottomless well of loss. I wait in silence, the wordless language of soul. My breathing slows down. I think I am falling asleep. Or am I? Perhaps I am slipping into unconscious numbing again? But I hear Laura inside me. "I came to you before in life. Now I come to you again in death. I am what I AM—invisible in living form, visible in living formlessness."

This natural communion on the threshold between form and formless embraces me with an all-encompassing Love. The experience of me as a body transforms into a super-saturated solution of Divine Love. My heart is heavy with personal love and loss, yet part of me is light, spacious, wordless and free from deeply ingrained habits patterned into my brain-body. The Love that remains is all that I am. It is not of me, nor of Laura. It creates itself as Presence permeating all the spaces between objects, inside objects and inside me. I begin to believe that the core of death, the eternal flame, the burning fire of sun-radiance, ignites the physical world into a manifesting Being. All I can do is weep, yet, inside my weeping, I experience the silent joyous laughter so typical of living Laura. The soundless sound bubbles throughout my whole being, like rose-colored sparkling champagne.

17

THE TRANSFORMATIVE NATURE OF DEATH

"There is a love so vast that no matter how far you travel you cannot step out of its circumference."

–Rainer Maria Rilke

"Heavy is the root of light."

–Tao te Ching

Spring 2016

Two years ago today we scattered Laura's ashes on the island. Time seasons my grief, making it more digestible. Reflecting on those days, I realize that as her youthful body began to fade in incremental shifts, I too began to fade. When the cells in her body lost their capacity to absorb living nutrients, I lost my capacity to engage.

Parts of my personality fell away. I lost interest in former values, percepts, and materialism. My attraction to them withered away into a silent, dark void. I was empty space, a hole inside the fabric of the whole. I was released from self-images. I stayed with this silence. My grief dissolved in the silent abyss as a gnawing hole of motherlove. Still born, my attention lingered inside a mute reservoir of intelligent w/holeness.

Absorbed into death qualities, transparent, nothing, there remained peaceful rhythmic breath, free of physical limitation and the story of me. Like waves unfolding upon a shore, the eternal pattern of rising, hovering, falling, dissolving, stillness and reforming, established a sense of stability and predictability inside the movement of earth's seasonal life cycles.

Even now, Laura's physical death transforms me. I remember the morning she lifted her head to look at her water-logged legs and football feet. She didn't recognize her body, yet she was fully aware. She said, "How curious, Mom. Have I been in an accident? I guess dying is the next experience for me to explore."

She withdrew her energy from the outer world to re-center in interior space equally real and alive. Her words from her fire of cremation, "Love me as I AM, not as I was," echo through me today. Who am I to love now that she is dead? Old voices echo in my mind: "Don't go there! It will kill you. You will be annihilated." What is this familiar, catastrophic impulse that makes me anxious and tired of the burdens of life?

Breathing in the anxiety, another impulse silently makes its sensate presence known. Lightly weighted and free of effort, awareness expands into a spherical form. My attention becomes stable with greater sensitivity and clarity. Intimate tenderness emanates from a core of light, a center capable of loving my woman's body.

Like Grandmother Oak tree, flesh life absorbs earth's strength and simultaneously opens into sky. I am created inside this great love affair between particles condensing into substance while opening into boundless space—a pulse of life, the pattern of breathing.

Inside the space of breath, awareness is freed from feeling separate. A natural resting point unveils a dimension of open, spacious, clarity. Everything within the space shares aspects of a dynamic whole. A deep intimate knowing awakens. The knower within subjective experience is the same knower in spacious clarity. However, in spaciousness the experience of a body is undefined aware space free of my personal history. I am a field of tender love where eternal wisdom breathes me into presence. I exist as a molecule of human consciousness awakening in a female body that is beautiful with spiriting LIFE.

Indestructible as gravity, the core-self infuses me with silent strength, capable of accompanying Laura from life to death and into the beyond. A newly realized quality of humble courage accepts that I could not save Laura from death, nor can I save myself from mine. I am free.

I feel responsible to bring this confluent play of form and formlessness awareness into my daily life. Living inside the temple of the ordinary, a term coined by wise friends, I am home in the world and also home in the eternal. I cannot prove this, but I can live the mystery inside the unfolding now and know I AM that.

In her final weeks, Laura spoke only of love. After long periods in deep meditation, where she lay in perfect stillness to avoid unbearable pain, she would open her eyes, turn her head ever so slightly to look into mine and say: "You must tell"…and she would say a name—Melissa, John, a cousin, a friend, a colleague—"that I love them. You must tell them, Mom." I felt she was planting seeds into their hearts, into their beings where fresh roots of an emerging awareness was growing. The evolutionary process of expanding consciousness was opening up into another way of knowing, creating a new ring of awareness, beyond the familiar range of ego reality.

The transformative nature of death awakens a spark of still born Life, intimately known and present. Perhaps a spark of Life didn't die with Laura's physical death, but rather flickered and jumped into another dimension with a unique way of communion like the warmth of the sun.

A voice speaks: "I came to you before in life. Now I come to you again in death. I am what I AM—invisible in living form, visible in living formless space."

"A cloud never dies."

–Thich Nhat Hanh

18

W/HOLY BEING

"The goal of life is to make your heartbeat match the beat of the universe, to match our nature with Nature."

–Joseph Campbell

"To the discerning man, all instincts are holy."

–Friedrich Nietzsche

Laura's loving joy never died. The impersonal nature of the Great Love infused her personal heart when she accepted death in her still-living flesh. When I walk in nature, swim in the lake or dance spontaneously, I sense Laura's life essence. In the unconditioned nature of subtle sensibility, my joy in movement and my great love for being alive perfume my experience. These universal qualities, I realize, are within me, yet, when I sense-feel the qualities of Laura's joyous love, I discern a discretely nuanced expression, unique to her energetic nature. I feel her soul essence inside my inner space. I resonate differently, same yet different. When I recognize her imprint of joy and love, my inner being smiles, 'Ah, there you are,' and I sense-feel a distant 'yes' echo through open fields hidden in the marrow of my bones. Then I know Laura died as a person: then I realize the beautiful soul qualities she lived and strengthened during her dying days, deeply imprinted into the collective soul in her friends, in me, and perhaps in all humankind. Her soul qualities dynamically merge to remain alive in the universal field of living, spirited matter.

I do not wish to transcend the weight of birth; rather, I choose to develop ego skills necessary to function responsibly. Instinctual fears for self-survival remain to protect me. I respect my physical limitations. At the island I am passionate about kayaking. I wear my life jacket and leave my route on the counter. On wild, windy days, I explore the back bays and small channels; on calm, clear days, I paddle far out into the open waters. When negative self-talk loops through my brain, I pull harder on my paddle, deepen my breath and increase my heart rate. When I synchronize my breathing with a steady rhythmic paddle, my brain shifts out of the merged perspective and familiar monkey mind. I stop paddling to silently rock on the water's surface. Balanced in the center of my tiny, royal-blue craft, seagulls assume I am one with them. Sometimes a monarch butterfly flutters near me on its flight to a distant shore. Stillness calms me. The natural world soaks into my heart and flows harmoniously with the free qualities of sky, water and space. I am sparkling with Life. A super-saturated reality of indivisible Divine Life permeates my consciousness. The sense of separateness fades into the background. A tiny, open hole, a pinprick of intimate awareness awakens within the fabric of indescribable wholeness. Doing nothing, qualities of the harmonious whole seep through the hole within this living whole—I am w/hole.

Nothing in me wants to change what I am, feel and live. In the silence, my heart whispers, "You are that and that and this is here and now, still born of flesh."

"Adore and love the One with your whole being, and the One
will reveal to you that each thing in the universe is a vessel,
full to the brim, with wisdom and beauty. Each thing the
One will show you is one drop from the boundless river of
infinite beauty."

–Rumi

225

ACKNOWLEDGEMENTS

Still Born would not be a book without the tender support of family and friends. My beloved husband, John, grieving in his own way for Laura, grew deeper into my bones. During our many years of marriage the resonance of mutual sensitivity and respect expanded into a capacity to walk hand in hand into the fire of death. With his red teacher's pen, he clarified using simpler language, the more abstract nature of pure awareness. Our dearest daughter, Melissa, Laura's big sister, supported us emotionally. Her marriage to Erich coupled with sharing their home and two children, Winona and Rowan, kept us in the loop of joyous living.

With my limited computer skills, Diamond Fotiadis came to my aide to create a single file out of the 25 chapters I recorded from my painful journals. I sent the rudimentary draft to my writing group: Kathy Berg, Sandi Caplan, Ardath Finnabogason-Hill and Catherine Heighway. These four wise women, writers and artists themselves, labored through the original material, made many perceptive suggestions and helped shaping my ramblings into moments of insight. When writing and editing the material over a period of nine years, the small Inquiry Group I am part of, Teresa Bryant, Mary Joy MacDonald, and Deanne Pederson, continued to ask me deepening questions about the essence of my experience.

My continued correspondence with a few friends from the Marion Woodman Foundation—mystics, meditators, Buddhists, therapists, and analysts— encouraged me to delve deeper into the invisible reality of silence, dreams, visions, and non-dual reality. When writing and editing *Still Born*, my connection to unseen dimensions, first encountered in 1980 with Martin Mueller, never left my background awareness. I trusted that the veiled dimensions would fundamentally shift my knowledge base about everyday living. When my intuitive cousin, Wendy Hilliard, sent me a photo of Laura stepping into the water, the title: *Still Born: Stepping into the Unknown* spontaneously appeared.

When I sent the manuscript and photo to Catharine Clarke, dear friend, editor, and writer, she promised me she would create something beautiful to offer others. Her subtle suggestions for deeper clarification, along with her understanding of the formless nature of some of the material, helped her fulfil her promise to me.

It is clear to me now that the creation of *Still Born* was a group project created out of a great love of all LIFE. I am deeply grateful to you all.

ABOUT THE AUTHOR

Mary Hamilton, M. Ed. is a classically trained dancer and graduate of the National Ballet School of Canada. A pioneer in movement education, she innovated the first full credit dance courses for High Schools in Canada during the 1970s. For many years she taught Modern Dance, Improvisation and Choreography at the University of Western Ontario. From 1980 to 2017, Mary co-created and team taught the internationally known BodySoul Intensive Workshops, first offered through UCLA Extension and later through the Marion Woodman Foundation. Her publications include: *Leaving My Father's House: Journey to Conscious Femininity*, co-authored with Marion Woodman (Shambala, 1992), *Under the Horse's Ass: A Love Story Human and Divine* (Colenso Island Press, 2000), and *The Dragonfly Principle: An Exploration of the Body's Function in Unfolding Spirituality* (Colenso Island Press, 2009). In *Still Born: Stepping into the Unknown*, Mary delves deeper into the exploration of the emerging consciousness of oneness.

HOW TO ORDER

Still Born - Stepping into the Unknown: A Memoir of Dying with My Daughter is available at Amazon and other online retailers. It can also be ordered from your favorite bookstore.